Multimedia Storytimes

Robin Works Davis

Alleyside Press®

Fort Atkinson, Wisconsin

Published by Alleyside Press,
an imprint of Highsmith Press LLC
Highsmith Press
W5527 Highway 106
P.O. Box 800
Fort Atkinson, Wisconsin 53538-0800
1-800-558-2110

Copyright © by Robin Works Davis, 2000
Cover design: Debra Neu Sletten

The paper used in this publication meets the minimum requirements of the American National Standard for Information Science — Permanence of Paper for Printed Library Material. ANSI/NISO Z39.48-1992.

Library of Congress Cataloging-in-Publication Data

Davis, Robin Works, 1962–
    Multimedia storytimes / Robin Works Davis.
      p. cm.
    Includes bibliographical references.
    ISBN 1-57950-028-5 (pbk. : alk. paper)
    1. Language arts (Early childhood)--Audio-visual aids. 2. Language arts (Early childhood)--Computer-assisted instruction. 3. Storytelling. 4. Internet (Computer network) in education. 5. Libraries--Nonbook materials. I. Title.

LB1139.5L35 D395 2000
372.6--dc21
                                          99-053292

Contents

ⓔⓔⓔⓔⓔⓔⓔⓔⓔⓔⓔⓔⓔⓔⓔⓔⓔⓔⓔⓔⓔⓔⓔⓔⓔⓔⓔⓔⓔⓔⓔⓔⓔⓔⓔⓔⓔ

Introduction 5

Multimedia Programs 13

ABC 13

Alligators & Crocodiles 15

Ant-ics 17

Antlers 20

Apples 22

Australia 24

Birds 26

Bubbles 28

Buenos Dias 30

Butterflies 32

Buzz 34

Cajun Fun 36

Dolphins 37

Egg-citing 39

Farm Life 41

Flies 44

Friends Around the World 46

Frogs 48

Go Batty 50

Hedgehogs 52

How Does Your Garden Grow? 54

Human Body 56

Jobs 58

The Jungle 60

Lovely Lizards 62

Lucky Leprechauns 63

Native Americans 65

No Ghosts 67

Nuts 68

Penguins 70

Pigs 72

Pirate Pals 74

Sign Language 76

Squiggly Wiggly Tales 77

Starry Night 79

Tooth Fairy 81

Trains 83

Turtle Tales 85

Wiggle and Hop 87

Zoo Doings 89

Multimedia Index 91

Introduction

ⓒⓒⓒ

Multimedia Storytimes has been written for the many librarians, teachers, parents and caretakers who are excited about using computers and multimedia to teach and delight the children they work with. Here you'll find practical suggestions, creative activities and complete storytime programs that incorporate different types of media into 40 story hour themes.

We all know children love hearing stories simply told by the traditional teller, but many schools and libraries now have the equipment to offer multimedia segments worked into storytimes or in the language arts setting. This book is intended to aid teachers and librarians in selecting, evaluating and using multimedia appropriate for children ages three through seven. Through the books, multimedia, related activities here and an open learning environment children will develop their imaginations as well as increase their thinking skills, computer use skills, and pre-academic skills.

How to Use This Book

This introduction has lots of collected ideas and resources to help you put together great multimedia programming. The first section, More about Multimedia, provides background information on multimedia, what it is and how it can be used as a learning tool for young children. This is followed by Getting Started, a variety of hands-on check lists to use in preparing your first multimedia programs. These include evaluation, equipment and planning outlines to make preparation easy. The last section, Related Issues, has material on information literacy and filtering, very important topics that we are learning more about all the time.

The main body of the book consists of 40 themed programs. I have tried to keep these simple, direct and easy-to-use. Each story program is arranged around a theme that begins with a CD-ROM or website. Each includes:

- WWW Internet sites and CD-ROMs
- Film and video – Length in minutes is provided.
- Bibliography – Including fiction and nonfiction. Award winners that are generally well known are

not included unless they are especially appropriate to the theme.

- Crafts and activities
- Songs, song books, fingerplays, rhymes and music recordings

For all of the themes, there were many books and media materials to choose from. The programs I created do not have exhaustive resource lists, but rather, selective collections made with the time restrictions of most storytime programs in mind, usually 30 minutes. All selections offered were chosen because they extend the theme in some unique way. I hope you enjoy these and find materials that work for you!

Keeping Current

One thing is true about the Internet—it will continue to change. To help keep you current on the websites listed in this publication, we will post any changes and new links at a dedicated website established for this book: www.hpress.highsmith.com/rwdup.htm. You can also reach me through this website with any questions or suggestions. I will look forward to hearing from you.

More about Multimedia

What Are Multimedia Resources?

Educational resources are divided into two primary categories—print and non-print. Before the development of the personal computer, non-print resources consisted of films, filmstrips, audio recordings in a variety of formats, slide sets and realia. More recent media include videocassettes and laserdisks. The personal computer introduced a wider range of resources, including educational computer software, CD-ROMs, educational databases, DVDs (digital video disks), the World Wide Web, and many other new formats containing digitized information and instructional resources. Some resources such as CD-

ROMs and the Web can offer video clips, animation, live action, and sound segments. Others offer interactive learning opportunities, where children can create their own learning path through a virtual tour, a visit to the zoo or maybe through an animated safety village.

This book focuses primarily on videocassettes, CD-ROMs, and websites because these are the most commonly available resources. However, bear in mind that some of the CDs and websites may contain a variety of other media, in addition to being interactive. For the sake of simplicity, we refer to all of these varied learning formats as multimedia.

Further, even though the purpose of this book is to offer creative activities that strengthen skills in using multimedia, we have included recommended books related to the program topics and activities that are commonly available in schools and libraries. Multimedia is of growing importance, but we believe that reading and books are still critical to every child's development.

Why Use Multimedia Activities?

The growing variety of multimedia has added a new dimension to learning. And as research begins to accumulate on its use, mounting evidence shows children who play with computers, the Internet, and other media may be stimulated to learn more than those who do not.

In 1993, Seymour Papert wrote about the use of computers with children in the book *The Children's Machine: Rethinking School in the Age of the Computer*.[1] Papert compares the idea of isolating computers in labs to the body's immune response to a foreign intruder. By isolating computers in areas away from where children are and what they enjoy, it is effectively minimizing the potential impact that computers can have on children's learning. Children need more access to computers for them to fully affect their learning experiences. It is a fatal flaw to remove computers from a child's daily routine, as they will think of it separately and information will be quickly outdated. Only when computers are truly integrated as a vital element in children's learning and applied to real daily activities with real purpose will children gain the most valuable of computer skills they need: the ability to use computers as natural tools for learning.[2] Using multimedia also provides an extra element of motivation to kids. The sounds, text, and visuals of multimedia offer multiple ways for children to pay attention. The interactive quality of most . animated products allows children to take a two-dimensional story and manipulate the media into another dimension.

What Kind of Multimedia Motivates Children the Most?

Here are some key points to consider when incorporating technology:

- Does the multimedia add value to the storytime? Try not to use merely textual or tutorial multimedia.
- Does the multimedia promote good listening? Fingerplays, rhythmic activities, and repetitive songs sharpen listening skills. Technology should add to this experience.
- Does the multimedia encourage creativity and allow children to move through and beyond listening to share responses and interact to sounds, words, and graphics?
- Does the multimedia link reading, responding, and computer use in an effective way?

How Do You Use Media in Programming?

Christine Miller, Children's Librarian at the Dupont Branch of the Allen County Public Library in Indiana has been using multimedia in her storytimes for about three years. She uses multimedia in several ways, but never for more than five minutes in a 30-minute storytime. The following are some of her experiences:

"When doing a storytime about monkeys or some other animal, I might use a product such as *Mammals* to show the children pictures or short video clips of the animal and to provide sound effects. Sometimes at the end of a storytime, I use *Bailey's Book House*. We would make up our own story as a group and play it back. This was especially nice to do with visiting daycare groups because we could print it out, and they could take it back to their center.

When doing a storytime on weather, I would often use the Weather Machine on *Sammy's Science House* and we would "design" our own weather and explore different weather conditions. Likewise, for storytimes about seasons, we would go to the pond in *Sammy's Science House* and watch the seasons change and explore the differences.

I sometimes use Internet sites. Recently I did a storytime about pets and at the end I invited the children to join me at a computer to explore the Blue's Clues site—a big hit! We explored the site for a few minutes and then printed out the coloring pages.

While I have occasionally used a Living Book such as the Arthur stories, I find it works best if I use a contained segment, such as a song or a game that is included in the story—instead of going through the story on the computer."

What Can You Accomplish with Multimedia?

Successful educational multimedia programs do the following things:

1. *Encourage learning.* Good multimedia programs encourage users by offering supportive words and additional chances to select correct responses. This exploration and experimentation empowers children as learners.

2. *Foster Independence.* Children using good multimedia can take responsibility for what they learn and the choices they make. Self-directed decisions lead to a higher motivation for learning.

3. *Offer Variety.* The best multimedia programs offer a wide range of levels of difficulty, making it accessible to a large audience. This also allows the child to grow and learn with the program through the levels.

4. *Offer Assessment.* Most educational multimedia offers some sort of assessment, such as onscreen rewards (known as animations or "stickers") and encouraging messages.

5. *Engage the Child Visually and Verbally.* As a child learns to read, they associate words and pictures with words. Color, sounds and action accompany graphics in multimedia programs. Children can hear stories read, watch animations, click on words, sentences or paragraphs.

6. *Provide Entertainment.* Even the best multimedia program does no good if the child doesn't enjoy it. It must engage them right from the first screen with activities that are fun.

Getting Started

In order to plan your multimedia storytime you will need to spend time getting the right equipment and resources together. To make that easier I have provided tools for selecting and evaluating the equipment and materials needed.

Helpful Hints

Preparation: Take a special storytime session to familiarize your group of children with the computer. Point out, demonstrate and let them interact with the various parts, such as the keyboard, mouse, etc. Encourage them to listen closely and be alert for the use of the computer's features and components during the coming story sessions.

Multimedia: As much as possible allow children in your group to interact with the CD-ROMs and Internet sites suggested for the programs. Choose several children each time to manipulate the mouse or punch the keyboard with your assistance. Let kids come to the screen and point out objects or selections of the computer images on the screen. If this is not possible, during demonstrations allow as much discussion and interaction with the materials and you as possible. If you are sharing a CD or online story, it might even be better to turn off the sound and share the stories aloud yourself. Let the children know you are reading off the screen, point out details of images, and encourage chiming in of repetitive refrains just as you would when sharing a book.

Patterns: There are many patterns throughout this book that can be enlarged on a photocopier to be used as coloring sheets. These can also be copied and traced onto heavier paper and used as storytime name tags. Punch holes in the shapes and add yarn for the children to wear like a necklace or tape them to the children's shirts.

Crafts and Other Activities: As time allows, involve the children in coloring, cutting and assembling of the activities. The key is to engage them so they have a memorable and meaningful experience. If it is not possible for time's sake, then give the children the materials they will need in the most ready state possible. Consider a rolling supply cart with packets of needed materials that get passed out when it is time to do an activity. If space is limited, a supply station can be created on a bulletin board—staple or tack up envelopes, paper cups or small boxes to hold precut papers, crayons, etc.

Multimedia Storytime Program Checklist

Several Months Prior to Event

> Develop Objectives for storytimes.
> Decide on themes/topics for storytimes.
> Identify available resources.
> Purchase needed resources and equipment.

One Month Prior to Event

> Obtain permission from administration.
> Assemble materials and make final selections.
> Set up and test equipment.
> Identify audience, date, and time.
> Begin publicizing event.
> Check websites and see if the links are still available.
> Develop contingency plan with an alternate date and alternate activities in case of equipment problems.

Two Weeks Prior to Event

> Schedule equipment assistance if needed.
> Set up equipment and do a dry run of program with multimedia.
> Bookmark websites to be used in storytimes.
> Determine seating arrangements and equipment arrangements.

Day Prior to Event

> Assemble materials.
> Prepare seating.
> Prepare and re-test equipment.
> Prepare decorations, displays, exhibits, crafts and handouts.

Day of Event
    Check facility.
    Lighting.
    Temperature.
    Room Arrangement.
    Equipment cords.
    Greet guests.

After the Event
    Do informal evaluation.
    Do formal evaluation.
    Begin planning next program.

Evaluating Multimedia

Selection and evaluation of media is made so much easier by the review sources and checklists that have been created in the last few years. If you do not have a system in place for your school or library, or just want to update what you've been using, there are a number of key points and great sources listed here. Sometimes it is easier to work from a checklist, and with this in mind, I've included sample forms on pages 9 and 10. Generally, most multimedia, including CD-ROM and Internet sites, should be evaluated based on the following checklist:

- Does the multimedia in question have real, interesting content, or is it only a list of facts or links?

- Is the Information contained accurate and free from bias?

- Who is the author? Is the author or creator identified, credible, and knowledgeable in the area?

- Is the content user friendly and easy to navigate?

- Is the information accurate?

- How does the site or CD-ROM compare with others on the same subject?

- Is the information well written?

For Internet sites:

- How well is the site maintained?

- Does the site tell you when it was last updated?

- Is there a mechanism for feedback on the site?

- Do the links on the site work?

- Does the site require additional software or hardware?

- Do the graphics, video, or audio add value to the site?

Evaluation Resources

For more detailed information on multimedia selection criteria, see the following sources.

Alexander, Jan, and Marsha A. Tate. *Web Wisdom: How to Evaluate and Create Information Quality on the Web.* Lawrence Erlbaum, 1999. For more information see: <www.erlbaum.com/html/ 2066.htm>

American Library Association. Seven Hundred Great Sites: Selection Criteria. <www.ala.org/parentspage/greatsites/ criteria.html>

Grassian, Esther. Thinking Critically about World Wide Web Resources. <www.library.ucla.edu/ libraries/college/ instruct/web/critical.html>. Questions are divided into topics such as Content &Evaluation, Source & Date, etc.

Hunt, Chance, and Judy Nelson. "Multimedia Storytimes," *Booklist*, May 15, 1996: (1596–1597).

Kirk, Elizabeth E. "Evaluating Information Found on the Internet." <milton.mse.jhu.edu:8001/research/ education/net.html>

Rettig, James, and Cheryl LaGuardia. "Beyond 'Beyond Cool': Reviewing Web Resources." *Online* 23, no. 4 (July/August 1999): 51-55.

Internet Sources for CD-ROM Reviews and Purchase

CD-ROM Guide
http://cd-rom-guide.com/index.html
Has 32,000 comprehensive annotations for CD-ROM and commercial software. Includes prices and company.

Internet Software Shop
http://www.shoplet.com/software/html/search.html
Offers 60,000 software titles for purchase. Has product notes for some titles, but not all. Includes pricing and product descriptions.

Kids Domain Software Review
http://www.kidsdomain.com/review/index.html
Reviews, articles, and columns written by parents, educators and staff. Over a thousand software reviews.

Moondog Multimedia
http://www.moondog-multimedia.com/play.html
Reviews of new CD-ROM products written by staff.

Electronic Resource Product Checklist

Product Description

Date _____   Name of Product _____

Vendor_____   Phone _____

Address _____

Subject _____

Age Level_____   Is there a printed counterpart? _____

How is the electronic source different from the print resource? _____

_____

What related resources are available? _____

_____

Are there published reviews of this product available? _____

Technical Considerations

Does the product run on presently owned hardware? _____

If not, what hardware is needed? _____

Is any other equipment needed? _____

Is there a toll free hot line or customer service line provided by the vendor? _____

Product Costs

What is the initial cost? _____   Is there a need or a charge for updates? _____

Website Evaluation Form

Site Name: _____   **Site Address:** _____

Author: _____   **Date Visited:** _____

Directions: _____

There are no editorial review boards responsible for information published on the Internet. It is essential that you learn to review websites critically. Below are some questions that will help you evaluate websites and the information found on them. Look at each website carefully and answer the questions with a yes or no and then add your own comments.

Design	Yes/No	Comments
Is the site visually appealing?		
Does the site use features like sound and video that maximize the Internet's potential?		
Do the graphics enhance the site's content?		
Do the internal and external links work properly?		
Is the material well organized?		
Navigation		
Is it easy to move around the website?		
Are there clear choices about how to find more information?		
Can you navigate within the site without getting lost?		
Does the site have an internal search engine?		
Authority (Author)		
Is it easy to determine the author of this website ?		
Are sources cited?		
Is there a link to the author for questions/feedback?		
Content/Accuracy		
Does the page title reflect its content?		
Do the authors clearly state their objectives?		
If so, did the authors meet their objectives?		
Is material updated frequently with revision date visible?		
Is the information unbiased and balanced?		
Are authors forthright about particular views/agenda?		
Did the site enhance your knowledge of the subject?		
Does the site provide information not readily available from other sources?		

Recommended Equipment

If you want to take full advantage of the Internet and multimedia, you must determine whether you have the right computer hardware and software you will need. Using the Internet means that your computer must be capable of receiving text, graphics, pictures, sound, and video. Your computer must have a sound card, drivers, and specialized software. The following is the minimum equipment needed to use the multimedia activities included in this book.

Hardware: The brain of the computer is the Central Processing Unit (CPU) or platform. The platform should be at least a PC Pentium/60 processor, Macintosh or Power Mac with a minimum 16 megabytes of RAM (Random Access Memory) (32–64 megabytes preferred). This amount of memory is required for speed of access to the websites.

Computer monitor: 256 color, 15 " color VGA monitor for seeing the range of colors used on many sites for children.

CD/DVD Drive: Double speed (2X) CD-ROM or DVD drive is useful for quick access to images on CD-ROMs. The original 1X speed drive reads 75 sectors per second (a sector is 2K). The transfer rate, which is the time it takes to read a sector on a CD-ROM. The transfer rate on a 1X CD-ROM drive is 150K per second. The 2X CD-ROM drive doubles the transfer rate to 300K per second. The faster transfer rate allows for faster data retrieval and smoother motion in video clips. A DVD drive is somewhat faster and will work fine for CDs.

Sound capability and speakers: External speakers with Creative Labs Sound Blaster.

Video capability: 32 mb AGP video is recommended.

Mouse: A remote mouse is nice to have but is not a necessity.

Keyboard

Printer: A black and white printer is needed for some activities.

Modem: A modem, which is a hardware device that allows one computer to communicate with another computer via the telephone lines. Modems convert computer data into audio signals. Modems transfer information at varying speeds. You will need a modem that transfers a minimum 28,800 bits per second (bps). It takes a 28,800 bps modem about 70 seconds to transfer the equivalent of approximately 90 single spaced type written pages from one point on the Internet to another. A slower modem, such as a 14.4000 bps, will take about twice as long (141 seconds) to transfer the same amount of data.

Projection Equipment: An LCD (liquid crystal display) projection package, consisting of an LCD panel, overhead projector, all the appropriate cables and adapters is recommended for classroom activities and library programs. An LCD Data/Video or Multimedia Projector available from library supply catalogs, such as Highsmith, can also be used. These are quite a bit more expensive than the LCD package, but offer such features as a virtual or remote mouse and video compatibility. The purpose of the package or projector is to hook up to the computer that is being used and project the images from the Internet or CD-ROM on to a screen for viewing by a group. The images are projected in color.

Software: Macintosh System 7x, or Windows 3.1x or better. Make sure you purchase the correct software for your operating system.

A graphical Web browser that will accommodate multiframes format and Javascript, such as Netscape Navigator or Internet Explorer. Browsers permit you to search out documents that are linked together on the World Wide Web. Browsers are capable of presenting a variety of formats on the monitor or page of information, including sound, video, and interactive graphics.

Helper applications will be necessary to add to your selected browser for listening to audio files, viewing videos, and portable documents and such. Dial up connection to the Internet via an Internet Service Provider (ISP).

Related Issues

Information Literacy

Multimedia has added a new dimension to traditional information literacy issues. The following are ways in which multimedia can assist in meeting the information literacy standards developed by the American Library Association and the Association for Educational Communications and Technology.[3]

- Children learn about selecting and applying appropriate multimedia and technology for a task or problem. (Information Literacy Standard #1)

- Children learn about acquiring information from print, visual, and electronic sources. (Information Literacy Standard #1)

- Children learn to use or produce visual forms that enhance the impact of their product or presentation. (Information Literacy Standard #3)

- Children see the storing and recording of data in a variety of formats. (Information Literacy Standard #3)

- Children see a demonstration of the ethical use of resources and materials. (Information Literacy Standard #8)

- Children evaluate the significance of information and ideas presented in written, oral and visual form. (Information Literacy Standard #2)

Filtering

Librarians have been involved in evaluating and selecting collections according to patron needs, financial limit, and space restrictions for a long time. This time honored tradition, like so many others, is being questioned in the new Web environment. Arguments about access for children range from no Internet access to complete and open access for all in libraries.

Although a full discussion is far beyond the scope of this book, its importance cannot be overstated. Here are a couple of thoughts to keep in mind. Consider you library's purpose in making your decision. For example, a school library's purpose is generally educational. Libraries are only required to permit access to materials related to its purpose. If you use this argument, school libraries may be able to block certain Internet sites that do not coincide with their educational purpose. Libraries may also consider restricting access to sites that present criminal or liability issues.

There are two alternatives for controlling or restricting Internet access if you choose to do so:

- Allowing individual parents to offer guidance as they see fit. This means requiring parents to be present when children are using the Web.

- Installing Filters that block access to specific websites. When a blocked site in accessed, a message appears on the screen stating that it is blocked. Some of the software is preset and some can be customized.

Filtering Software Choices

Cybersitter

Cybersitter offers what is called "intelligent phrase filtering." Cybersitter considers the context in which words are written. Cybersitter will also automatically block all sites from Internet service providers that have personal Web pages by users that contain adult or other objectionable content. Cybersitter can also keep a log of information that is sent out over the Internet from the computer on which it is installed. Find out more at http://solidoak.com/cybersitter

SurfWatch

Surfwatch from Spyglass Software blocks known adult sites and sites that have "sex," "XXX," or "porno," as part of their Internet address. Surfwatch is available for both Windows and Macintosh. Find out more by calling 1-800-677-9452.

Net Nanny

Net Nanny has a dictionary of keywords that can be customized. It includes a starter dictionary of 1,000 words, which is updated monthly though Web downloads. Find out more at http://www.netnanny.com/netnanny/home.html.

Cyberpatrol

Cyberpatrol allows adults to limit the amount of time a child spends online. The program also filters twelve categories of sites, such as sex, hate speech and violence.

Notes

1. Papert, Seymour. *The Children's Machine: Rethinking School in the Age of the Computer.* Basic Books, 1993.
2. Shade, D. D. and J. A. Watson, "Computers in Early Education," *Journal of Educational Computing Research*, 6 (4), 1990: 375-392.
3. American Library Association and the Association for Educational Communications and Technology. *Information Power: Building Partnerships for Learning.* ALA, 1998.

ABC

Getting Started: Multimedia ABCs

A great way to start a multimedia storytime series is to focus on the alphabet. There are so many excellent CDs and websites about the alphabet, it will allow you to demonstrate right off the variety that is available to children and the appropriateness of the selected items' content.

Internet Site: Sesame Street Alphabet

www.ctw.org/preschool/printme/character/0,1157,2163,00.html

Click on any letter and see a picture with a related sentence to read aloud. Site from Children's Television Workshop.
[4 min.]

A Is for Alligator

A is for alligator,
Crunch, crunch, crunch.
(scissor arms open and closed)

B is for bounce,
Bounce a bunch.
(jump up and down)

C is for circle,
Go round and round.
(turn around)

D is for dizzy,
Now sit down.
(sit)
[Action Rhyme—I min.]

Book: *Over Under in the Garden: An Alphabet Book*

A beautifully illustrated picture book with full-page paintings of plants, animals, vegetables, and insects depicted in alphabetical order. By Pat Schories. Farrar, Straus & Giroux, 1996.
[3 min.]

ABC

Leader: I said A, B, C.
Everyone repeats: A, B, C.
Leader: I said A, B, C.
Everyone repeats: A, B, C.
Leader: I said A, B, C, D, E, F, G!
Everyone repeats: I said A, B, C, D, E, F, G!
Leader: Uh-huh!
Everyone repeats: Uh-huh!
Leader: Oh, yeah!
Everyone repeats: Oh, yeah!
Leader: One more time.
Everyone: A, B, C, D, E, F, G
And H, I, J, K, L, M, N, O, P!
Leader: Q, R, S!
Everyone repeats: Q, R, S!
Leader: T, U, V!
Everyone repeats: T, U, V!
Leader: X, Y, Z!
Everyone repeats: X, Y, Z!
[Chant—4 min. to teach/I min. to perform]

CD-ROM: *Chicka Chicka Boom Boom*

Listen to the story with the rhymes and songs. Macmillan Media. [story]
[5 min.]

CD-ROM: *Animal Parade*

Ninety-eight animals form a parade to represent the letters of the alphabet. By Jakki Wood. Bradbury, 1994. [story, activities]
[3 min.]

Internet Site: Alphabet of Animals

www.infostuff.com/kids/a.htm

This page starts with "A is for Angelfish." Click on back or next to see more letters. Let kids select animal cartoon pictures to print and take home. Site from Infostuff.
[I0 min.)

Additional Resources to Share

Books

Brown, Ruth. *Alphabet Times Four*. Dutton, 1991. The alphabet depicted in four languages—English, Spanish, French and German.

Jahn-Clough, Lisa. *ABC Yummy*. Houghton Mifflin, 1997. An alphabetical tour of good things to eat.

Johnson, Stephen. *Alphabet City*. Viking, 1995. Paintings of objects in urban settings depict the letters of the alphabet.

Red Hawk, Richard D. *A, B, C's: The American Indian Way*. Presents the letters from A to Z, using each letter to introduce the culture, customs, and history of North American Indians.

Video

Richard Scarry's Best Video Ever. Golden Video, 1989. 30 min. The alphabet is acted out by Miss Honey's class in a sweet and interesting way, with each student introducing a letter and telling a story about it.

CD-ROM

A to Zap. Sunburst. Go to the Alphabet Room and click on the letters you choose work with. Follow the directions and do the related activities. [activities}

Alphabet Express. School Zone. Choose a letter, then try to find all the objects that begin with that letter in the bedroom. Then go to the Firehouse and play the letter matching game. [alphabet games, activities]

Chicka Chicka Boom Boom. Macmillan Media. This version of the well-known alphabet story also contains music and games. Listen to the story with the rhymes and songs. [story]

Curious George's ABC Adventure. Houghton Mifflin Interactive. This CD includes a story with interactive games. Select "I Spy a Butterfly" and sort objects by first letter sounds. [story, games]

Internet Sites

Children's Television Workshop: Big Bird's ABCs. **www.ctw.org/parents/safari/article/0,1121,7789,00.html** Go on a safari with Big Bird! One of the activity sets from the Parents Toolbox series.

Cybermom: Alphabet **http://wneo.org/cybermom/abc.htm** This site has several activities to introduce children to the alphabet, sound blends, simple words, and other concepts.

Enchanted Learning: Little Explorers Picture Dictionary **www.enchantedlearning.com/Dictionary** This dictionary contains over 1,300 illustrated entries, most with links to related websites. Just click on a letter of the alphabet and see pictures of words that begin with that letter.

Alligators & Crocodiles

Setting the Scene: Create a Swamp

Create a "swampy" area by placing a blue sheet or table-cloth on the floor. Lengths of brown felt or cloth can be logs, or bring in real logs for kids to sit on. Play a cassette with swamp sound effects, such as *Everglades* from Music Company. Use the pattern on page 16 to make alligator coloring sheets.
[3 min.]

Internet Site: The Wild Ones

www.thewildones.org/Animals/gator.html

Learn about the American Alligator and compare photos of alligators and crocodiles. Site from the Wildlife Preservation Trust International.
[2 minutes]

Alligator

Here is an alligator, *(right hand forms head)*
Sitting on a log. *(right hand on left arm)*

Down in the pool, *(make a circle with arms)*
He sees a little frog. *(look down in arms)*

In goes the alligator, *(dive with arms)*
Bump goes the log.

Splash goes the water, *(put arms up in air)*
Jump goes the frog. *(jump)*
[Fingerplay - 1 min.]

Book: *Rockabye Crocodile: A Folktale from the Philippines*

Two wild boars learn lessons about being kind from a mother crocodile. By Jose Aruego. Greenwillow, 1988.
[5 min.]

Did You Ever See an Alligator?

(Tune of "Did You Ever See a Lassie?")

Did you ever see an alligator,
An alligator, an alligator?
Did you ever see an alligator
With great big sharp teeth?

He's big and he's mean
And oh, so green.
Did you ever see an alligator
With great big sharp teeth?
[Song—1 min.]

Internet Site: Wild Sanctuary

www.wildsanctuary.com/frameset.html

Alligator sound effects are available at this site. Go to the "Sound Safari" section and choose number 4.
[4 min.]

Five Little Monkeys

Five little monkeys in a tall tree, *(hold up five fingers)*
Old Mr. Crocodile can't catch me! *(shake head "no")*
Along comes Mr. Crocodile and *SNAP!*
(hold one arm up and the other down and snap together)

Four little monkeys. *(hold up four fingers)*
Repeat with 4, 3, 2, 1, and "No more."

What Mr. Crocodile did not know,
He was allergic to monkeys and so...
Achoo! Achoo! Achoo! Achoo! Achoo!
As you can see, five little monkeys back in the tree.
[Action Rhyme—2 min.]

Activity: Alligator Bookmark

Enlarge the alligator pattern below, copy onto stiff paper and cut around the outline. Let each child color their own. Punch a hole in one end with a hole punch and add a yarn tassel. This pattern can also be used to make stick puppets to act out the fingerplay.
[10 min.]

alligator pattern for bookmark

Additional Resources to Share

Books

Christelow, Eileen. *Five Little Monkeys Sitting in a Tree.* Houghton Mifflin, 1991. The popular children's rhyme featuring monkeys and an alligator is illustrated.

Eastman, P.D. *Flap Your Wings.* Random House, 1969. A proud pair of birds try to raise a baby crocodile to be a bird.

Moselle, Shirley. *Zack's Alligator,* HarperCollins, 1989. Zack receives an alligator keychain that seems to have magical growing powers.

Video

Alligators All Around. Weston Woods. 4 min. From the book by Maurice Sendak, alligators have a jamboree with antics for each letter of the alphabet.

CD-ROM

Alligators: Appetite to Zigzag! Carole Marsh Family. Interactive information about alligators, crocodiles and habitat. [factual information]

Amazing Animals. Dorling Kindersley Multimedia. Explore with Henry the Lizard. Look at crocodile and alligator photos. [factual information, activities]

American Heritage Children's Dictionary Multimedia Edition. Houghton Mifflin. Type in the words "alligator" and "crocodile." Listen to the words pronounced and look at the animation of the alligator or crocodile moving, swimming or eating. [reference]

Internet Sites

The Birmingham Zoo: American Alligators
www.zoomwhales.com/subjects/Alligator.html
Alligator facts and photos to see.

Enchanted Learning: All About Alligators
www.zoomwhales.com/subjects/Alligator.html
Alligator information, including pictures to print, sounds to hear, and background information about the evolution and habitat of today's alligators.

alligator pattern for coloring sheet

Ant-ics

Setting the Scene: Ant Bulletin Board

Before the program, make a giant paper ant colony on a bulletin board or wall. Cover the area with brown paper. Cut out "tunnels" from white or ivory paper place on the brown base. When the children arrive, have them cut out ants from red and black paper using the pattern on page 19. Give them pipe cleaners for antennae and legs to give their ants a three-dimensional look. Have the children place their ants in the colony. Make Ants at the Picnic nametags using the pattern on page 18.
[10 min. for children's activity]

Internet Site: The Ant and the Grasshopper

www.umass.edu/aesop/ant/index.html

An online version of *The Ant and the Grasshopper* that contains unique and original illustrations. From Scott Roberto, art student at the University of Massachusetts.
[3 min.]

I'm an Ant

I'm an ant
And a gi-ant—
To an ant,
But
I'm an ant
To a giant.
[Rhyme—1 min.]

Book: Effie

Effie's loud voice annoys everyone until she saves the other ants and earns their respect. By Beverley Allinson. Scholastic, 1990.
[5 min.]

Ants

Once I saw an anthill with no ants about,
So I said, "Dear little ants won't you please come out?"
(cup hands over mouth and talk to the ground)

Then as if the little ants had heard my call,
1, 2, 3, 4, 5 came out and that was all.
(hold up fingers on one hand in succession)
[Fingerplay—1 min.]

Book: *Two Bad Ants*

Two bad ants desert their colony until a dangerous adventure shows them where they belong. By Chris VanAllsburg, Houghton Mifflin, 1988.
[6 min.]

Game: The Ants Go Marching

Form a big circle and walk around as you sing the song "The Ants Go Marching." For large groups, have children break into twos, threes, etc., while still walking in a circle—finding their own partners or groups. When they can't find a group of ants to march with, they sit out the rest of the game. The game ends when groups of ten are formed. For small groups, simply march single file while singing.

The Ants Go Marching

The ants came marching two by two, Hurrah! Hurrah!
(students walk in pairs side by side each other in a circle)
The ants came marching two by two
The little one stopped to tie his shoe.
They all go marching down around the town.
Boom, Boom, Boom.

Additional verses:

The ants came marching three by three...
The little one stopped to climb a tree.

The ants came marching four by four....
The little one stopped to shut the door....

The ants came marching five by five...
The little one stopped to take a dive....

The ants came marching six by six....
The little one stopped to pick up sticks....

The ants came marching seven by seven....
The little one stopped to go to heaven...

The ants came marching eight by eight...
The little one stopped to shut the gate...

The ants came marching nine by nine...
The little one stopped to scratch his spine...

The ants came marching ten by ten
The little one stopped to say *the end*!
[Song—10 min.]

Internet Site: The Ants Go Marching

www.enchantedlearning.com/rhymes/Ants.shtml

Read a rebus of the song. Site from Enchanted Learning.

[4 min.]

☼ Additional Activity: Giant Ants

Use toothpicks to connect two Styrofoam balls and one Styrofoam egg (for the three body parts of the ant.) Insert six pipe cleaners into the Styrofoam for the legs. Bend the pipe cleaners to look like the ant is walking. Paint ants red or black. When dry, glue on googly eyes and there's your giant ant! For a simpler craft, use the ant pattern (p. 19) to copy, cut and make stick puppets.

Additional Resources to Share

Books

Climbo, Shirley. *The Little Red Ant and the Great Big Crumb*. Clarion, 1995. A small red ant thinks she is unable to lift a crumb, so she enlists the help of various other animals.

Losi, Carol. *The 512 Ants on Sullivan Street*. Scholastic, 1997. A cumulative rhyme in which the number of ants who appear doubles each time another treat is set out on the picnic blanket.

Video

Magic School Bus: Gets Ants in Its Pants. PBS, 30 min. Ms. Frizzle and the gang explore an ant hill.

CD-ROM

The Big Bug Alphabet Book. Millican Publishing. Use the CD in the "Let Me Play" mode to see the bugs in this story sing. [interactive story]

Disney's Active Play: It's a Bug's Life. Disney Interactive. Play a scavenger hunt to help Flick repel the grasshoppers from ant island in this story CD based on the movie. [games]

Eyewitness Children's Encyclopedia. Dorling Kindersley Multimedia. Go to the article on ants and share the pictures and information with the children. [factual information]

Internet Sites

Discovery.com: The Ultimate Guide to Ants www.discovery.com/stories/nature/ants/ants.html Kids can look at live pictures of an ant farm through the Ant Cam, see ant videos, talk to an ant expert, and check out the best ant sites on the Web.

nametag pattern

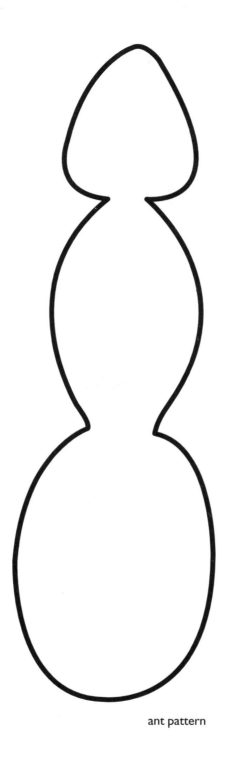

ant pattern

Antlers

Activity: Thumbprint Antlers

Give each child a picture of the moose without antlers on page 21. Set out inkpads and baby wipes. Tell the children to create thumbprint antlers on their pictures.
[5 min. or more]

Internet Site: Moose Tales

www.northstar.k12.ak.us/schools/upk/moose/moose2.html

Stories and drawings of "moose encounters" by a third grade class. Site from University Park Elementary School, Fairbanks, Alaska.
[3 min.]

Moose

One baby moose standing in the snow,
Waiting for his mother so they can go.
Next came a buck with antlers tall,
And to the forest he gave a moose call.
What is this in the forest I see?
Two more babies, that makes three.
[Fingerplay—1 min.]

Book: *Mucky Moose*

Mucky Moose lives in the swamp and is so smelly that he scares off a wolf. By Jonathan Allen. Simon & Schuster, 1996.
[5 min.]

Moose

Moose march slow, *(march in place)*
Moose tippy toe. *(tip toe in place)*
Moose marches to and fro. *(march forward and back)*
Moose march fast. *(march in place quickly)*
Whoa, moose, whoa! *(stop)*
[Action Rhyme—1 min.]

Book: *Salt Hands*

A gentle tale of a girl who befriends a stag in the middle of the night. By Jane Aragon. Dutton, 1989.
[6 min.]

Shy Deer

One mama deer, standing near a tree.
(hold up one finger)
Two baby deer hiding, quiet as can be.
(hold up two more fingers)
I quietly watch shy deer,
And they watch me.
(point to self)
[Fingerplay—1 min.]

CD-ROM: *American Heritage Children's Dictionary*

Type in various animals that have antlers, such as moose, deer, antelope, etc. Listen to each one's name pronounced and watch the animations. American Heritage. [reference]
[3 min. or more]

✪ Additional Activity: Book

Mooses Come Walking

A 12-line, finger-snapping rhyme accompanied by acrylic paintings of moose antics. By Arlo Guthrie, Chronicle Books, 1994.

✪ Additional Activity: Antler Headband

Enlarge the antler shape below and cut from brown construction paper. Cut a strip of poster board long enough to fit around a child's head. Staple the antlers to the poster board and tape the poster board to fit the child's head.

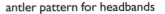

antler pattern for headbands

Additional Resources to Share

Books

Fox-Davies, Sarah. *Little Caribou*. Candlewick, 1996. A story that introduces the biology of animal life through that of a caribou.

Ritchie, Rita, and Jeff Fair. *The Wonder of Moose*. Gareth Stevens, 1992. Simple text and photos introduce this huge animal of the north woods.

Waddlell, Matin. *What Use Is a Moose*. Candlewick, 1996. This silly book tells the pros of having a moose for a pet.

Song

"You Might See Some Deer" from *Animal Piggyback Songs* by Jean Warren. Warren, 1990.

Video

Bell on a Deer. Pied Piper, 15 min. A fawn is frightened by an eagle and gets separated from its mother. Mei, a kind little girl, finds the deer and they have many happy adventures together.

CD-ROM

Mars Moose. Lightspan Partnership. Do activities with Mars Moose on this CD of stories and games, such as listen to a "Liquid Book" read aloud. [games, activities]

Internet Sites

Cariboo Moose Productions: Cariboo Kids
www.ilap.com/songs/bcard.htm
Make a "Happy Moosday" card by printing the page and following the instructions.

Southern Living: Rudolph Cookies/Magic Reindeer Food
www.southernliving.com/thismonth/december/kids.asp
Directions for making cute reindeer cookies with pretzel antlers, and also for making magic reindeer food.

True Friends Have Fun: The Magic Berry Patch
http://userdata.acd.net/smith.judy/TFMB.htm
Online story of a girl, a deer and a magical berry patch. By Levant Smith.

The Wilderness Society: Deer Coloring Sheet
http://earthday.wilderness.org/kidsstuff/deer.htm

moose pattern

Setting the Scene: All About Apples

Investigate different varieties of apples, such as Golden Delicious, Red Delicious, Jonathan, and Winesap. Bring some of these to taste test with your group. Share the book *How to Make Apple Pie and See the World* by Marjorie Priceman, (Knopf, 1994). Use an atlas to point out the different places the narrator travels to. Use the pattern on this page to make apple nametags or enlarge it for a coloring sheet.
[10 min.]

Apple Tree

Here is the apple tree with leaves so green,
(make leaves with outstretched fingers)
Here are apples in between.
(make fists)
When the wind blows,
(blow)
The apples will fall,
(drop fists to the ground)
But here is a basket to catch them all.
(form basket with arms)
[Action Rhyme—1 min.]

Internet Site: Apple Corps

http://apple-corps.westnet.com/apple_corps.2.html

Play with the virtual apple as you would a "Mr. Potato Head." Site from Chris Rywalt.
[5 min.]

Little Apples

(Tune of "Ten Little Indians")

One little, two little, three little apples,
Four little, five little, six little apples.
Seven little, eight little, nine little apples,
All fell to the ground.
[Song—1 min.]

Book: *The Apple Pie Tree*

Describes an apple tree as it grows, from leaves, to flow-ers, to fruit, and also a family of robins that lives in its branches. By Zoe Hall. Scholastic, 1996.
[4 min.]

Apple Poem

Apples big,
(make large circle with arms)
Apples small,
(make small circle with hands)
Guess what?
I love them all!
(hug yourself)
[Action Rhyme—1 min.]

CD-ROM: *A World of Plants*

Look at the photos and listen to the story about the apple tree. National Geographic. [story, factual information]
[7 min.]

✿ Additional Activity: Thumbprint Apple Tree

Pass out copies of the tree pattern on page 23 and let the children color the trunk with crayons. Using a non-toxic red stamp pad, let the children use their thumbs to stamp red apples on the trees. Next they can use crayons to fill in the leaves.

pattern for apple nametag or coloring sheet

Additional Resources to Share

Books

LeSeig, Theo. *Ten Apples Up on Top.* Beginner Books, 1961. The classic rhymes tell about three animals competing to see who can balance more apples on their head.

Macmillan, Bruce. *Apples: How They Grow.* Houghton Mifflin, 1997. A photographic essay on apple trees and how they bear fruit.

Rockwell, Anne. *Apples and Pumpkins.* Simon & Schuster, 1989. A family tells of its fall ritual of going to a farm to pick their own apples for pie and pumpkins for jack-o'-lanterns.

Video

Johnny Appleseed. Rabbit Ears. 25 min. Video tale of the benevolent seed-planting rambler, John Chapman.

CD-ROM

Dole 5-a-Day Adventure. Dole Food Company. Play with the animated apple and learn about fruits on this CD full of facts about fruits and vegetables. [factual information, activities]

Granny Applebee's Cookie Factory. Micrographics Software. Run Granny Applebee's cookie factory, following recipes to make "cookies" and fix cookie machines. [cooking]

The Magic Apple House. Thompson Learning. Kids will get some business "basics" while they learn to launch an apple growing business using functions such as cutting, pasting, and filing on the computer. [activities]

Internet Sites

Dole Food Company: Just for Kids
www.dole5aday.com/menu/kids/menu.htm
Choose "apples" from the Fruit and Vegetable Encyclopedia to learn cool things about apples.

Johnny Appleseed Inc.: Johnny Appleseed Home Page
www.richmond.edu/~ed344/webunits/khistory/johnny appleseed2.html
Join the kids club and learn about ecology, apples, and being thrifty.

Washington State Apple Commission: Apple Cards
www.apples.org/postcard/index.html
Send an apple card with music to a friend.

pattern for thumbprint apple tree

Australia

Activity: Australian Animal Matching Game

Cut duplicate sets of Australian animals out of magazines such as *National Geographic*. Select and show each child an animal picture. After the child has seen and recognized the animal, tape it face-down on their shirt. All the children then move around the room behaving as they think the animal in the picture on their shirt might act. The object of the game is for the children to locate the other child who has a picture of the same animal.
[5 min.]

CD-ROM: *World Walker: Destination Australia*

Go on a Walk About. Click on animals to learn their names or look at the reference library for animals and Australia. Includes video, sounds, and maps. Soleil Software.
[5 min.]

Five Tiny Emus

Five tiny emus, wishing they could fly.
One ran away after taking a try.

Four baby emus, looking for their mom,
One went to find her and he was gone.

Three baby emus bother a kangaroo,
One jumped in her pocket and now there are two.

Two baby emus hear a kookaburra call
One got scared, now there's one, that's all.

One little emu didn't want to be alone,
So he said "Squawk!" and went right home.
(hold up fingers for 5-4-3-2-1)
[Fingerplay—1 min.]

Book: *Australian ABC*

A smorgasbord of native Australian animals, from A to Z. By Colin Theile. Weldon Kids, 1993.
[4 min.]

Have You Seen a Koala?

(Tune of "Do You Know the Muffin Man?")

Oh, have you seen a koala, a koala, a koala,
Oh have you seen a koala,
That lives in Australia?
[Song—1 min.]

Book: *One Woolly Wombat*

A witty, colorful counting book of Australian animals. By Rod Trinca. Kane Miller, 1985.
[5 min.]

Kangaroos

Five baby kangaroos all in a row,
(hold up five fingers)
When they see their mother they kick just so.
(kick)
For their mother they have missed,
So they hop up and give her
A great big kiss, *SMACK!*
(hug self and make kissing sound)
[Fingerplay—1 min.]

Craft: Kangaroo Puppets

Reproduce the kangaroo pattern on page 25 on brown paper and laminate. Cut each kangaroo out and attach the leg with a paper fastener. Tape to a craft stick. When the puppet is moved up and down, the leg will move as if it is hopping.
[10 min.]

Additional Resources to Share

Books

Catterwell, Thelma. *Sebastian Lives in a Hat.* Kanmi Press, 1995. Sebastian is a wombat adopted by a kind human family and his favorite place is inside a woolly hat.

Fox, Mem. *Possum Magic.* Abingdon, 1983. Baby possum is made invisible by possum magic, and he and grandmother possum must travel all over Australia to find a cure.

Video

Joey Runs Away. Weston Woods. 8 min. From the book by Jack Kent. After Joey the young kangaroo runs away, other animals try out his mother's pouch while she searches for him.

CD-ROM

Blinky Bill's Ghost Cave. Dreamcatcher Interactive. Listen to the tale of Bill, the dingoes, and rabbits. [story]

Kevin the Kangaroo. Animations Software. Learn all about a kangaroo family in the Australian bush with an aboriginal boy named Namatjira. [story]

My First Amazing World Explorer. Dorling Kindersley Multimedia. Point and click on the model of Australia, do activities, and look at pictures. [factual information, activities]

Internet Sites

Australian National Botanical Gardens: Australia's Flag
www.anbg.gov.au/images/flags/australia.gif
An illustration of Australia's flag.

Enchanted Learning: Zoom School Australia
www.EnchantedLearning.com/school/Australia/
This site has a map, folk song, flag, craft, story and animal information related to Australia. Click on any of these items.

Pittsburgh Zoo: Kangaroo Pictures and Information
http://zoo.pgh.pa.us/wildlife/grey_kangaroo.html
Information and photos of the grey kangaroo. By Janice Frazier, Zoo Instructor.

Wangaratta Primary School, NE Victoria, Australia
www.ozemail.com.au/~wprimary/kooka.htm
Kookaburra picture and sound.

pattern for kangaroo puppets

Birds

Activity: Make a Bird

Using the pattern on page 27, cut out a bird outline from poster board and have the children color eyes, beak, etc. Finish by gluing craft feathers on the birds.
[10 min.]

Internet Site: Round Bird Can't Fly

www.pacificnet.net/~cmoore/roundbrd/15.htm

Online story about a bird who really wants to fly but can't because of his big, round body and little wings. Site from Carole Moore.
[6 min]

Little Bird

I saw a little bird go hop, hop, hop.
(hop in place)
I said to the bird, "Stop! Stop! Stop!"
(hold hand up flat like stop sign)
I went over to say, "How do you do?"
(bend at waist)
Wiggle, waggle went his tail and away he flew!
(form bird with hands and make it "fly")
[Action Rhyme—1 min.]

Book: *Have You Seen Birds?*

A simple description of various types of birds, their sounds and activities. By Joanne Oppenheim. Scholastic, 1986.
[4 min.]

Five Robins

Five robins in a sycamore tree,
Father, *(thumb)*
Mother, *(index)*
And babies three. *(remaining fingers)*

Father brought a worm, *(point to thumb)*
Mother brought a bug, *(point to index)*
And the three babies started to tug.

This one ate the bug, *(point to middle finger)*
This one ate the worm, *(point to ring finger)*
And this one sat and waited his turn.
(point to pinkie finger)
[Fingerplay—1 min.]

Book: *Beaky*

An egg tumbles to the jungle floor and hatches, but the bird is unaware of his own identity until a frog helps him out. By Jez Alborough. Houghton Mifflin, 1990.
[5 min.]

Internet Site: Grace Bell Collection

www.rbcm.gov.bc.ca/nh_papers/gracebell/english/call_plo.html

www.rbcm.gov.bc.ca/nh_papers/gracebell/english/call_ww.html

Let the children listen to the unusual calls of the Plover and Winter Wren at these sites. Sites from Royal British Columbia Museum.
[4 min.]

Five Squawking Parrots

Five squawking parrots in a line on the floor,
One flew away and then there were four.

Four squawking parrots flew up to a tree,
One ate a coconut and then there were three.

Three squawking parrots living at the zoo,
A fine lady bought one and then there were two.

Two squawking parrots basking in the sun,
One got a sunburn and then there was one.

One squawking parrot left all alone,
His mother called him and then there were none.
[Fingerplay—1 min.]

✪ Additional Activity: Feather Paintings

While playing a selection of bird songs or a classical piece such as "Nightingale Serenade," have the children make paintings using feathers as brushes. Encourage them to describe the feelings they have through line and color. Use 18"x 12" construction paper as a surface. Tell them they may use either end of the feather as the brush.
[15 min.]

Additional Resources to Share

Books

Dunbar, Joyce. *Baby Bird*. Candlewick, 1998. A cumulative tale that follows Baby Bird's first steps, flight, and flops.

Rockwell, Anne. *Our Yard Is Full of Birds*. HarperCollins, 1992. Describes the many birds that visit a yard, from crows, to wrens.

Video

Cat and Canary. Weston Woods. 5 min. From the book by Michael Forman. A city cat who lives out his fantasy of being able to fly decides that staying on the ground isn't so bad after all.

CD-ROM

Junior Nature Guides: Birds. APG. Play the knock-knock bird jokes. [factual information, activities]

Multimedia Bird Book. Workman Incorporated and Swift International. Help photographer Everly Glades take photos for the magazine *The Birder*. [factual information, interactive activities]

Shelly Duvall's It's a Bird's Life. Sanctuary Woods. A 60-screen story of a bird's journey from Los Angeles to the Amazon rain forest. Click on "character" to learn about birds. [story, factual information]

Internet Site

Enchanted Learning: All About Birds
www.enchantedlearning.com/subjects/birds/Allaboutbirds.html
See pictures of a falcon, diagram of a feather, find out what birds eat, hear a song, and much more.

bird pattern

Bubbles

Setting the Scene: Dancing Bubbles

Play soft music as the children arrive for storytime. Then divide them into groups of three. Tell them to slowly and gently spin and "float" like bubbles. Tell them to float and drift together forming groups by joining hands. They can make larger and larger bubbles by joining with other groups. Continue to dance until you yell "Pop!" On "pop" the children all scatter.
[3–5 min.]

Internet Site: Bubble Puzzle

www.kidsdomain.com/down/pc/bubblepuzzlep1.html

Demonstrate this free downloadable game for your PC. Game by Conmeg Spielart. Available from Kids Domain.
[4 min.]

Book: *Monster Bubbles: A Counting Book*

Funny monsters count from one to ten by blowing bubbles. By Dennis Nolan. Prentice Hall, 1976.
[5 min.]

Super Bubble

(Tune of "Clementine")

Super bubble, super bubble
Watch me blow it in the air.
Wind is blowing
Bubble floating
Watch it burst
Right over there.
[1 min.]

Bubbles

(Tune of "Old MacDonald")

B-U-B-B-L-E-S,
Bubbles everywhere.
Toothpaste bubbles in my mouth,
Shampoo in my hair.
With a bubble here, and a bubble there.
Here a bubble, there a bubble,
Everywhere a bubble bubble.

B-U-B-B-L-E-S,
Bubbles everywhere.
[Song—1 min.]

Book: *Clifford Counts Bubbles*

Clifford the small red puppy counts from one to ten while playing with bubbles. By Norman Bridwell. Scholastic, 1992.
[3 min.]

Internet Site: Bubble Trouble

www.ambrosiasw.com/Products/BT.html

Download this freeware and play a game of "Squish the Fish" in a goldfish bowl full of bubbles. Site from Ambrosia Software.
[4 min.]

Here's a Bubble

Here's a bubble,
(make a circle with fingers on one hand)
And here's a bubble,
(make a circle on other hand)
And a great big bubble I see.
(make a large circle with arms)
Are you ready?
Let's count them,
1, 2, 3. *(repeat above actions)*
[Action Rhyme—1 min.]

Activity: Giant Bubbles

To make giant bubbles you will need a wading pool, hoola hoop, liquid dish detergent, glycerine (available at pharmacies), bath towel, and bricks. Put the towel in the pool and put the bricks on top of it. Fill the pool with about three inches of water. Add the detergent and glycerine, using four teaspoons of glycerine and one cup of detergent per gallon of water. Have a child stand on the bricks and swish the hoop in the water. As the hoop is quickly lifted, it will form a giant bubble around the child.
[7 min. or more]

Craft: Bubble Wands

Give each child a pipe cleaner and let them create their own bubble wand. They can twist them into hearts, diamonds, or any other shape. Make bubble juice from 1 gallon of water, 1 cup of regular blue Dawn dish detergent, and 4 teaspoons of glycerin.

CD-ROM: *Zoo Explorers*

Find the hidden tokens with pictures of animals throughout the game. Click on one and drag it over to the Bubble Machine to make it start. Learning Adventures. [games]

Additional Resources to Share

Books

Hooks, William et al. *How Do You Make a Bubble?* Bantom Doubleday, 1992. Rhyming tale that includes bubble gum.

Schubert, Ingrid. *The Magic Bubble Trip.* Kane Miller, 1985. A magic bubble carries a boy to a land of hairy frogs.

Winer, Yvonne, and Carol McLean-Carr. *Never Snap at a Bubble.* Educational Insights, 1987. Despite warnings by his parents, a baby frog snaps up too many bubbles.

Video

Let's Give Kitty a Bath. Weston Woods. 12 min. From the book by Steven Lindblom. Two children try to give kitty a bath, and a humorous chase ensues.

CD-ROM

Bubblegum Machine. Heartsoft. Earn pieces of bubblegum by matching rhyming words.

Water Works Balloon Bundle. GT Interactive Software. Go to "Freddi Fish and Luther's Water Worries." Luther thinks he can out-swim the bubbles as they float to the water's surface. Have the kids move the mouse to make Luther race the bubbles. [games]

Internet Sites

Exploratorium: Professor Bubble's Bubblesphere
www.exploratorium.edu/ronh/bubbles/bubbles.html
Learn all about bubbles, from their shape to what happens when two bubbles meet. This site also contains links to additional websites about bubbles.

The Thinking Fountain: Bubble Geometry
www.smm.org/sln/tf/b/bubblegeometry/bubblegeometry.html
This site, from the Science Museum of Minnesota, has plenty of information about bubbles such as the science of forming them, how they keep their shape, and more.

Buenos Dias

Setting the Scene: Where Is Mexico?

Bring out a globe or map of North America and show it to the children. Point out your location and point out Mexico. Discuss how long it would take to get to Mexico by car or airplane. Play music recorded by a mariachi band.
[5 min.]

Internet Site: Juegos y Canciones para los Niños

www.hevanet.com/dshivers/juegos

This site, from kindergarten teacher Doug Shivers, contains a section with songs and games in Spanish. Listen to one of the songs, then have the children sing along.
[6 min.]

Pretty Little Clown (El Lindo Payasito)

Look who approaches, a jolly little clown.
Let's do what he does and sing or jump around.
(One child is the Little Clown, and does actions of his own choosing, such as clapping, stamping, etc. The rest of the children mimic him.)
[Song—I min.]

Book: *Borreguita and the Coyote: A Tale from Ayutla, Mexico*

Borreguita the sheep constantly outwits the wolf until the wolf finally leaves the area. Translated by Verna Aardema. Knopf, 1991.
[7 min.]

Los Colores (Colors)

I see rojo as the fire at night. *(red)*
I see the sky as azul and bright. *(blue)*
I see cafe in coffee cups. *(brown)*
I see negro spots on little pups. *(black)*
I see verde as the grass. *(green)*
I see gris as a swimming bass. *(gray)*
I see naranja as pumpkin seeds. *(orange)*
I see amarillo in dandelion weeds. *(yellow)*
No matter what color I seek,
It makes no difference what language I speak.
[Poem—I min.]

Book: *Hot-Cha-Cha!*

A story about Maria and her friends, who find a lost key to a city playground which leads them to a fun rhyming adventure. By Josephine Nobisso. Winslow, 1998.
[5 min.]

Internet Site: *Hot-Cha-Cha!* Activities

www.winslowpress.com

Click on "Book Titles" and *Hot-ChaCha!* to find activities to go with the book of the same name. Play "Kooky Jar" and listen to the salsa-beat sounds the jars make. Have the children try and repeat the sounds. Site by Winslow Press.
[4 min.]

Craft: Hanging Novio

Novios, or sweethearts, are symbols of tribute to loved ones used as decorations during Dia de los Muertos family celebrations. For novios, you will need pink tempera paint, a hole punch, yarn, scissors, a shallow paint tray, white poster board and masking tape.

Have each child dip one hand into a tray of pink poster paint. Have them make two imprints on a piece of poster board so that the fingers of the two prints touch and the palms angle out to form a heart, as shown below. After the paint dries, cut a heart shape around the print. Punch a hole in the top and add a loop of yarn.
[5 min. or more]

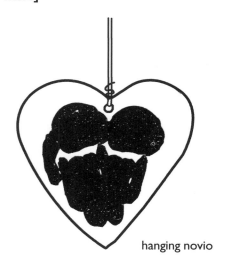

hanging novio

Additional Resources to Share

Books

Gonzalez, Lucia. *The Bossy Gallito*. Scholastic, 1994. A cumulative tale from Cuba about a self-centered Rooster trying to make his way to a wedding.

Johnston, Tony. *Dia de los Muertos/Day of the Dead*. Harcourt Brace, 1997. A Mexican family is described as it prepares for the Day of the Dead celebration.

_____. *The Iguana Brothers*. Blue Sky, 1995. Dom and Tom, the Iguana Brothers, eat flowers, pretend to be dinosaurs, and realize they are best friends.

Video

Isabelle in Mexico—Visiting the Mayas. Aims. 15 min. A young British girl visits a Mayan family in the Yucatan. She observes Mayan culture, harvests corn, plays, sees bows and flint-tipped arrows made by hand, and grinds grain to make tortillas.

CD-ROM

Games in Spanish. Syracuse Language Games. Learn vocabulary and pronunciation using a game modeled after Bingo. [games, language activities]

Jump Start Spanish. Knowledge Adventure. Mr. Hopsalot helps you explore a clubhouse in English and Spanish and sing Spanish folk songs. [language activities]

Ozzie's Travels: Destination Mexico. Digital Impact. Click on the projector and see a slide show about Mexico. [travel information]

Internet Sites

El Dia de los Muertos
www.inch.com/~lavender/diadelos.html
Lots of links, music, pictures and folklore about the Day of the Dead. Site by Catherine J. Lavender.

Butterflies

Setting the Scene: Butterflies in Cocoons

Before the program, make butterflies using paper egg carton sections for the body and construction paper for the wings. Use glitter, glue, markers, crayons, googly eyes and pipe cleaners to decorate. When you are finished, wrap the butterflies in white tissue paper as "cocoons" and close with a rubber band. Hang the cocoons around your story area. Show them to the children before you do the butterfly stories. When the stories are finished, have the children help you unwrap the cocoons to let the butterflies emerge.
[unlimited]

CD-ROM: *Cuthbert the Caterpillar*

Go on an adventure with Cuthbert and his two bug friends. The adventure ends with Cuthbert turning into a butterfly. MDI Publishing. [interactive story]
[5 min.]

Caterpillar

There was a little caterpillar crawling all about.
He worked and he worked without a doubt.
(wiggle index finger)

Wrapping himself in a snug cocoon.
Waiting and waiting … will it be soon?
(cover finger with other hand)

Look, he's coming out, my oh my!
Now he has become a beautiful butterfly.
(cross thumbs and let fingers be butterfly wings)
[Fingerplay—I min]

Book: *The Butterfly Kiss*

The butterfly flutters from creature to creature throughout the forest until he finds an unusual place to land. By Marcial Boo. Harcourt Brace, 1995.
[4 min]

Caterpillar Crawling

One little caterpillar crawling on my shoe.
Along came another and then there were two.

Two little caterpillars crawling on my knee.
Along came another and then there were three.

Three little caterpillars crawling on the floor.
Along came another and then there were four.

Four little caterpillars, watch them crawl away.
They will all turn into butterflies some spring day.
[Rhyme—I min.]

Internet Site: Thinking Fountain Monarch Page

www.smm.org/sln/monarchs/

Explore monarch butterflies and learn about their mysterious migration.
[5 min.]

Book: *Monarch Butterfly*

Describes the life, body parts, behavior, and life cycle of monarchs. By Gail Gibbons. Henry Holt, 1989.
[7 min.]

I'm a Caterpillar

(Tune of "The Addams Family")

Chorus:
My tummy is fat *(snap snap)*
I like it like that *(snap snap)*
I wiggle around,
I jiggle around,
My tummy is fat. *(snap snap)*

I'm a cat-er-pillar
I'm such a lovely fellow.
I love to eat and eat,
Those leaves are such a treat.
Repeat chorus.
[Song—I min.]

Activity: Butterfly Coloring Sheet

Enlarge the pattern on page 33 to make a butterfly coloring sheet. You can also use the pattern to make nametags.
[4 min.]

✪ Additional Activity: Butterfly Costumes

For each child, use a 24"x 36" piece of orange butcher paper. Fold the paper in half, draw a wing on it, and then cut out. Use large marshmallows (don't eat them!) and black and white tempera paint to sponge paint the wings. Let them dry. Staple two 2"x 9" pieces of black construction paper to two 9"x 12" pieces of black construction paper to form a bib, like the top of a pair of overalls. This will fit over the child's head, with the 2"x 9" pieces acting as straps. Staple the wings onto the back. Have a butterfly parade like they do in the book *Monarch Butterfly* by Gail Gibbons.

✪ Additional Activity: Butterfly Collage

Gather up quart-sized sealable sandwich bags, pipe cleaners, glitter, confetti, and strips of brightly colored crepe paper. Have the children fill the bags with collage items they want in their butterflies. Tell them to squeeze out any excess air as they close their bags. The sealable edge becomes the side of the butterfly's wing. Gather the bags in the middle, distributing an equal amount of collage materials on both sides. Pinch and wrap with a pipe cleaner to secure. Bend the pipe cleaner to form antennae. The butterfly is complete.

Additional Resources to Share

Books

Howe, James. *I Wish I Were a Butterfly*. Harcourt Brace, 1987 A cricket at Swampswallow Pond fails to appreciate his own beautiful song and wishes he were a butterfly.

Marzollo, Jean. *I'm a Caterpillar*. Scholastic, 1997. Simply describes life from a butterfly's point of view.

Video

The Caterpillar and the Polliwog. Weston Woods. 7 min. From the book by Jack Kent. A polliwog is so impressed by the bragging of a caterpillar that he decides to watch carefully so that he can turn into a butterfly himself.

CD-ROM

I Like Science: Butterflies and Moths. SVE. Watch the slides of moths and butterflies, then play the matching game. [factual information, activities]

Multimedia Bug Book. Workman/Swift Software. Click on the butterfly and then select the metamorphosis video clip. [factual information, activities]

A World of Animals: Butterflies. National Geographic/ Discis Knowledge. Choose to hear the story about butterflies. Also includes photos, facts and video clips. [factual information, story, activities]

Internet Sites

Bry-Back Manor Butterfly Activity Page
www.geocities.com/Heartland/6459/actpag36.html
An activity on the life stages of a butterfly. Site by Christine Rapuwolf.

Midcontinent Ecological Sciences Ctr: Children's Butterfly Site
www.mesc.usgs.gov/butterfly/butterfly-coloring.html
This site features pictures of a butterfly's life cycle to print out and color.

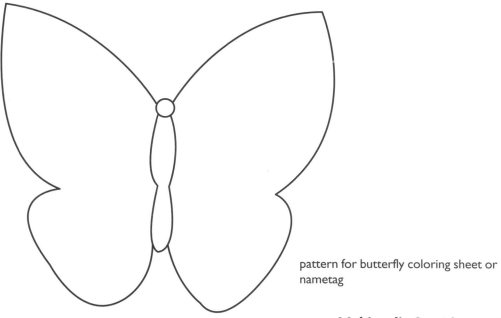

pattern for butterfly coloring sheet or nametag

Buzz

Setting the Scene: Celebrate Bees and Honey

What is the buzz on bees and honey? September is National Honey Month. Celebrate honey and honor it's producer, the honeybee. Use the pattern on page 35 to make nametags or enlarge and use as a coloring sheet.
[5 min.]

Internet Site: Bee Rhyme

www.enchantedlearning.com/rhymes/Bees.shtml

Read a rebus rhyme about bees. Site by Enchanted Learning.
[3 min.]

Book: *Honeybee's Busy Day*

Honeybee follows a winding path home to his hive in this book which features a removable bee character. By Richard Fowler. Harcourt Brace, 1994.
[6 min.]

Five Busy Bees

Five busy bees on a day so sunny.
Number one said, "I'd like to make some honey."
Number two said, "Tell me, where shall it be?"
Number three said, "In the old honey tree."
Number four said, "Let's gather pollen sweet."
Number five said, "We will take it on our feet."
(hold up five fingers and bend each one down)
[Fingerplay—1 min.]

Internet Site: B–Eye

http://cvs.anu.edu.au/andy/beye/descript.html

See the world through the eyes of a honeybee at B-Eye. Click on "gallery." Site by the Centre for Visual Sciences.
[5 min.]

Where Are the Bees?

Here is the beehive, *(make a fist)*
Where are the bees?
Soon they'll come flying out of their hive.
One, two, three, four, five. *(open fingers)*
Buzz-zz-zz!
[Fingerplay—30 sec.]

Book: *The Honey Makers*

Factual information is presented in an accessible format with great illustrations. Gail Gibbons. Morrow, 1997.
[6 min.]

Bumblebee

Brightly colored bumblebee
Looking for some honey.
Flap your wings and "buzzzzz" away
While it is still sunny.
[Rhyme—30 sec.]

Craft: Bee Puppet

Materials for each child

- yellow and tan construction paper
- scissors
- brown paper lunch sack
- glue
- black crayon
- 2 black pipe cleaners
- 2 buttons

Cut two yellow ovals from the yellow construction paper that are almost as wide and as long as the lunch sack. Glue one oval on top and one oval on the bottom of the sack to make the bee's body. Use black crayon to draw stripes on the yellow ovals. Cut wings from tan construction paper and glue one on each side of the bees body. Use the end of the pipe cleaner to poke two holes in the end of the body near the closed end of the bag. Stick the end of a pipe cleaner in each hole and twist it off to make antennae. Glue the buttons on as eyes.
[10 min.]

bee puppet

Additional Resources to Share

Books

Wallace, John. *Building a House with Mr. Bumble*. Candlewick, 1997. Flip and fold-out pages create a guessing game featuring a bumblebee.

West, Colin. *Buzz, Buzz, Buzz Went the Bee*. Candlewick, 1997. A buzzing bumblebee is told to buzz off by everyone except a butterfly.

Video

The Honey Bee: A Profile. Pied Piper. 12 min. This video introduces young children to the fascinating world of honey bees. It describes how they build their five, hibernate, care for their young, and make honey.

CD-ROM

Bug Adventure. Learning Adventures. Choose bees and watch the video. [factual information, activities]

A Bug in the Program. SWFTE International. Help Dr. Anson Pantz find his bugs that have escaped. Pick a habitat and look for the bee. [factual information, activities]

Elroy Goes Bugzerk. Headbone Interactive. Help Elroy find a bug for the bug race.

What's the Secret? 3M Learning Software. Send bees in search of pollen in this game based on the PBS show of the same name.

Internet Sites

Carol Moore: Buzzy Bee Online Story
www.magickeys.com/books/bee/index.html
Silly story of a bee who makes one too many stops to gather nectar. There is also a link to a Buzzy Bee coloring book.

Honey.com: Kids
www.honey.com/kids/index.html
This site contains honey bee facts, honey trivia, games and more. From the National Honey Board.

Quick Learn Software: The Beekeepers Home Page
http://ourworld.compuserve.com/homepages/Beekeeping
This page describes bees, honey and beekeeping with lots of bee-related links.

pattern for bee nametag or coloring sheet

Cajun Fun

Setting the Scene: Gingerbread Book and Treats

Read *The Cajun Gingerbread Boy* illustrated by Berthe Amoss (Hyperion, 1995). Move the cardboard gingerbread boy that comes with the book through the pages as you tell the story. Pass out Cajun gingerbread boys made with the recipe at the end of the story, or use purchased gingerbread treats.
[7 min.]

There Was a Little Lobster

There was a little lobster, *(make pinchers with hands)*
He lived in a box. *(make a box with hand)*
He swam in the ocean, *(make swimming motion)*
And climbed on the rocks.
(make one hand "climb" up other arm)
He pinched at a shrimp, *(make pinching motion)*
That swam in the sea.
He pinched at a fish, *(pinch again)*
But he didn't pinch me. *(shake head "no")*
[Fingerplay—1 min.]

Book: *Feliciana Feyda Le Roux: A Cajun Tall Tale*

Feliciana sneaks along on an alligator hunt and saves the day with her wooden doll. By Tynia Thomassie. Little, Brown, 1995.
[6 min.]

Internet Site: Looney Lobster's Travel Journal

www.vrml.k12.la.us/herod/library/journal.html

Read the journal entries of elementary students as they follow a lobster from Louisiana to Boston. Site by Heard Elementary School Library, Abbeville, Louisiana.
[4 min.]

Crawfish, Crawfish

(Tune of "My Bonnie Lies Over the Ocean")

Red crawfish live deep in the river,
And live on the floor of the sea.
Red crawfish live deep in the river,
I hope that they don't pinch me!

Crawfish, crawfish
They live on the floor of the sea, the sea.
Crawfish, crawfish,
I hope that they don't pinch me!
[Song—1 min.]

Internet Site: Cajun Music

www.louisianaradio.com

Click on "Listen to the Music" to hear a cajun tune. You'll need RealAudio Player, link offered at the site.
[3 min.]

Additional Resources to Share

Books
Collins, Sheila. P*etit Rouge: Cajun Twist to an Old Tale*. Pelican, 1996. A retelling of Little Red Riding Hood.

Reneaux, J.J. *Why Alligator Hates Dog*. August House, 1995. Dog tricks mean alligator into being chased by his human owner.

CD-ROM
Encarta Multimedia Encyclopedia. Encarta. Click on "encyclopedia articles" and type in "Louisiana." Click on "Zydeco music" to hear Clifton Chenier and the Creole Kings sing "Ay-Tete Fee aka Ehl Petite Fille."

Swamp Gas USA. Berkley Systems. Explore Louisiana and its landmarks as an alien in a flying saucer.

Travelrama. Berkley Systems. Look for parks and interesting sites in the state of Louisiana and earn a postcard.

Internet Sites
Écu Media Design: Encyclopedia of Cajun Culture
www.cajunculture.com
This online enclyclopedia provides basic information on Cajun-related topics such as language, culture, etc.

The Everyday Cajun Homepage
http://pcis.net/papabear
Click on "Cajun Scenes" to see photos of the swamp, boiled crabs, nutria and more.

Louisiana History: The Louisiana Legacy
www.geocities.com/BourbonStreet/Bayou/3055/legacy.html
Louisiana and Cajun stories, poems, jokes, pictures and recipes by kids.

Dolphins

Setting the Scene: Visit the Ocean

Collect a beach towel, umbrella, seashells, photos of dolphins, binoculars, and a recording of ocean surf. Set this up in your story area to look like a beach. Place the dolphin photos on the wall and let the children look through the binoculars, pretending they are "dolphin spotting" at the beach. A special treat is to make and serve blue Jell-o with crushed Oreo cookies on the bottom and gummy fish suspended in it. (The Oreos make the sandy bottom of the ocean.)
[5 min. or more]

Craft: Dolphin Nametags

Use the pattern on page 38 to make dolphin nametags. This pattern can also be enlarged and used as a coloring sheet.
[5 min.]

Internet Site: David's Whale & Dolphin Watch

http://neptune.atlantis-intl.com/dolphins/

Links, images and sounds of whales and dolphins. Select "To the Photos" for images or "Sounds" to hear how dolphins communicate.
[4 min.]

Book: *D Is for Dolphin*

An alphabet of dolphin-related words and objects. By Carri Berg. Windom, 1991.
[4 min.]

Dolphin

Little dolphin goes out to play,
(put one hand on top of the other with thumbs outstretched)
He wiggles his fins,
(wiggle thumbs)
Then swims away.
(make swimming motion with hands)
He swims and swims in the water bright,
Then opens his mouth to take a bite.
(keep hands together and open fingers like a mouth)
Mmmmm! Good!
[Action Rhyme—l min.]

Internet Site: Sea Creatures Mystery Game

www.mnps.act.edu.au/scm/scmttl.htm

Have kids try and solve these mysteries created by students at Mount Neighbor Primary School, Kambah, Australia.
[6 min.]

Book: *Waiting for Billy*

The true story of an unusual friendship between a dog and a dolphin. By Martin Jacka. Orchard, 1990.
[7 min.]

✪ Additional Activity: Fingerprint Dolphin

Enlarge and make copies of the dolphin pattern below. Gather gray tempera paint and foam paper plates or meat trays. Pour a little paint on the plates. Let children use their fingers to paint the dolphin with fingerprints. Use the pointer finger to paint the nose, tail, and lower fin. Use the thumb to paint the upper fin. Fill in the body with other fingerprints. Cut the dolphins out and hang with blue crepe paper streamers from a clothes hanger to make a mobile.

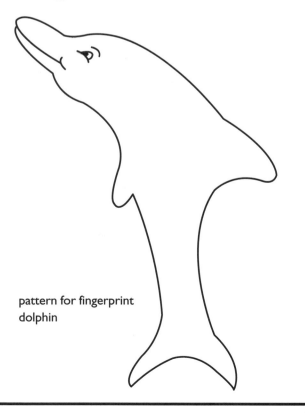

pattern for fingerprint
dolphin

Additional Resources to Share

Books

Farris, Diane. *In Dolphin Time*. Macmillan, 1994. A poetic, sparsely worded tribute to dolphins with blue-tinted photo montage illustrations.

Zoehfeld, Kathleen. *Dolphin's First Day*. Soundprints, 1994. Baby dolphins day from his birth to his first night is described.

Video

Dolphins, Our Friends from the Sea. Pied Piper. 13 min.

CD-ROM

Flipper Interactive Story Book. Brain Storm Software. Listen to the Flipper story based on the movie, and play the matching game. [story, games]

Me and My World. Future Vision. Choose the underwater scene, then click on the dolphin and watch the animation. [nature exploration]

Sea Creatures. PC Pig Multimedia Activity Kits. Activities about the sea and the animals that live there. Play the game and then make the dolphin puppet. [factual information, activities]

Seaside Adventure. Discovery Channel Multimedia. Explore the pages with Professor Iris and look for the dolphin. [factual information]

Internet Sites

Sea World: Dolphin and Me Coloring Page
www.seaworld.org/songs/dolphinandme.html
This page features a coloring sheet to print that identifies the body parts of a dolphin. Also contains a link to additional information on dolphins.

Whale Club Coloring Book
www.whaleclub.com/kids/dolphin1.gif
www.whaleclub.com/kids/dolphin2.gif
Dolphin pictures to draw and color.

pattern for dolphin nametag

Egg-citing

Setting the Scene: All About Eggs

Go to a local fair or farm and use a tape recorder to record the sounds of a poultry house to play for the children. Dress in overalls and carry a basket of plastic eggs. Surprise the kids by taking a stuffed dinosaur out of the basket. Tell them that dinosaurs also came from eggs. Have the kids think of other creatures that come from eggs and write down their responses.
[4 min.]

Internet Site: Introduction to the Amniota

www.ucmp.berkeley.edu/vertebrates/tetrapods/amniota.html

Which came first the chicken or the egg? Show the children a diagram of what is inside an egg.
[3 min.]

Counting Eggs

How many eggs does your basket hold?
(make a circle with your arm to the side)
1, 2, 3, 4, now put in some more,
(pretend to put eggs in basket)
5, 6, 7, 8, that's a lot, your doing great!
Get some more, try again,
Two more, that makes ten.
[Action Rhyme—1 min.]

Book: *Chicken's Aren't the Only Ones*

Vibrant illustrations and rhyming text presents the many animals that lay eggs. By Ruth Heller. Grosset and Dunlap, 1981.
[6 min.]

Five and Five

Five eggs,
(hold up five fingers)
And five eggs,
(hold up five more fingers)
That makes ten.
Sitting on top
Is a big mother hen.
(cup hands as if holding a hen)

Crackle, crackle, crackle,
(wiggle fingers)
What do I see?
Ten fluffy chicks
Smiling at me!
[Fingerplay —1 min.]

CD-ROM: *A World of Animals*

Go to the farm and see a chick emerge from an egg. National Geographic Software. [factual information]
[4 min.]

Video: *The Most Wonderful Egg in the World*

Weston Woods. To settle a quarrel between three hens, the king must decide which one lays the most beautiful eggs.
[6 min.]

Craft: Egg Coloring Sheet

Use the pattern on page 40 to make an egg coloring sheet. This pattern can also be used to make nametags.
[4 min.]

Additional Resources to Share

Books

Hein, Helme. *The Most Wonderful Egg in the World.* Atheneum, 1983. Three hens argue over who has the best egg, then go to lay eggs for the king and let him decide.

Hooper, Meredith. *Seven Eggs.* Harper and Row, 1985. In this lift-the-flap book, six different eggs hatch six different animals. The seventh egg contains a surprise.

Imai, Miko. *Little Lumpty.* Candlewick, 1994. A stretched-out, humorous version of the Humpty Dumpty rhyme.

CD-ROM

Green Eggs and Ham. Broderbund Software. Listen to the Dr. Seuss story. [story, games]

Zurk's Rainforest Lab. Soleil Software. Play "Egg Hunt" and help Nita the Lion Cub find twelve hidden eggs. [factual information, story, games]

Internet Sites

Enchanted Learning Software: Humpty Dumpty
www.EnchantedLearning.com/Humptyrhyme.html
Read the rhyme "Humpty Dumpty" in rebus.

National Geographic: Dinosaur Eggs
www.nationalgeographic.com/features/96/dinoeggs/
Look at dinosaur egg models.

The Science Museum of Minnesota: Thinking Fountain
www.smm.org/sln/tf/e/eggs/eggs.html
Learn about the life cycle of a Monarch beginning at the egg stage.

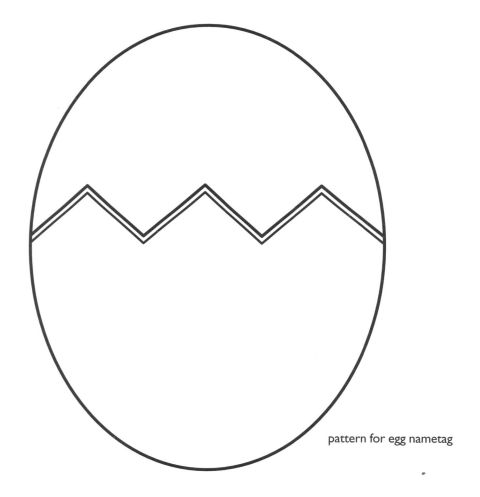

pattern for egg nametag

Farm Life

Setting the Scene: Let's Talk About Farms

Discuss the different kinds of farms and the products they produce, such as fruit, dairy products, or livestock. Play a game of farm animal charades to get the storytime started. **[6 min.]**

Internet Site: Barnyard Buddies

www.execpc.com/~byb/

On these pages you can color a picture on screen or watch an animated story about farm creatures. Site by the Stardom Company. **[4 min.]**

If You Were a Farmer

(Tune of "Did You Ever See a Lassie?")

Oh, if you were a farmer, a farmer, a farmer,
Oh, if you were a farmer, what would you do?

I'd gather eggs for breakfast,
For breakfast, for breakfast.
I would gather eggs for breakfast
That's what I would do.

(Repeat with "Milk the cows each morning," and "Feed the baby chickens.")
[1 min.]

Book: *Rockabye Farm*

A farmer rocks all of his animals and then his child to sleep. By Diane J. Hamm. Simon & Schuster, 1992. **[3 min.]**

Game: The Mixed-Up Animal Rhyme

Directions: Explain that animals have their own special languages. Each animal makes a special sound. In this game the animals are tricky—don't let them fool you and the farmer!

The Mixed-Up Animal Rhyme

A sheep and a chick and old brown cow,
Got together on the farm, and, wow, somehow
All their sounds got all mixed up,
And the worried farmer said, "Hey, what's up?"

Have flannelboard cutouts of various farm animals. Place a cutout on the flannelboard and say something like: "And the cow said *(build the suspense)*—Quack! Oh, is that right? Or is it all mixed up? What does the cow say? Moo, you're right! Poor farmer! What will he do with a cow that says quack?" Then go thru the other animals. Sometimes use the correct sound, sometimes a mixed-up sound. At the end go through them quickly again and make sure all the sounds are right. Then say, "…and the farmer was *so* happy … wouldn't you be?" **[3 min.]**

The Farm

The cows on the farm say "Mooo!"
The rooster says "Cock-a-doodle-doo!"
The horse says "Neigh!"
The sheep say "Baa! Baa!" all day.
The chicks say "Peep, peep, peep!"
The cat says "Purr," then goes to sleep.
The pig says "Oink, oink!" when it wants to eat.
And we say "Hello" to the animals we meet.
[Rhyme–1 min.]

CD-ROM: *Sitting on a Farm*

A multilingual reading and language arts product that has a story, writing, recording ability, music and songs in English, French or Spanish. Living Books. [story, activities] **[4 min.]**

Language Experience: Who Lives on a Farm?

This is an outstanding activity for teaching children tracking and one-to-one correspondence. You can use die cuts for the animals and the word "farm."

Make the following sentence on a sentence strip, leaving a space to place an animal die cut and room for the red barn at the end. I make a matching set of strips and cut them apart, so my students can match text in the pocket chart, or take words to their desks for writing.

A _____ lives on a (barn die cut goes here).

Animals to use include pig, cow, lamb, horse, dog, cat, mouse, duck, hen, rooster, rabbit, frog, and fish.

I also make individual student books of this story, from sentence strips with the shapes glued on. **[6 min.]**

Take Me Out to the Barnyard

(Tune of "Take Me Out to the Ball game")

by Judy Hall

Take me out to the barnyard.
Take me out there right now.
Show me the cows, pigs and horses, too.
I hear an oink and a neigh and a moo.

There are chickens laying their eggs.
If they don't lay, it's a shame.
Oh, it's one, two, three eggs today,
And I'm so glad I came.
[Song—I min.]

✪ Additional Activity: Put the Snout on the Pig

Cut a 15" circle from pink poster board. Cut two trian-gles from the pink poster board and tape them to the top of the circle to make ears. Use a black marker to draw eyes and a mouth on the pig. Cut 4" circles from pink construction paper and draw nostrils on them. Give each child a circle with tape and play "Put the Snout on the Pig" as you would "Pin the Tail on the Donkey."

✪ Additional Activity: Stick Puppet Story

Directions: Have the kids cut chickens out of construction paper from the pattern on p. 43 and glue on sticks. Or, use pictures from coloring books or other magazines.

Hens of a Different Color

This little hen is *BLACK* (*hold up black hens*)
She stands in the barnyard by a big hay stack.

This little hen is *RED* (*hold up red hens*)
She is very tired and won't get out of bed.

This little hen is *BROWN* (*hold up brown hens*)
She is feeling sad and wearing a frown.

This little hen is *YELLOW* (*hold up yellow hens*)
She's friends with the rooster; he's a handsome fel-low.

This little hen is *WHITE* (*hold up white hen*)
She dances and plays, oh what a sight.

This little hen is *PURPLE* (*hold up the purple hens*)
She spends her day running around in circles.

This little hen is *GREEN* (*hold up green hen*)
She is the silliest hen I've ever seen.

This little hen is *BLUE* (*hold up blue hen*)
She lays eggs for me and you.

This little hen is *PINK* (*hold up the pink hen*)
She goes down to the pond to get a drink.

All of these hens live at the farm
Out in the big *RED* barn.

✪ Additional Cooking Activity: Barnyard Salad

Encourage the children to think of food that farm animals like to eat and then create a salad. For example, rabbits like lettuce and carrots, horses like apples, and pigs love grapes. Use a yogurt or poppy seed dressing.

✪ Additional Cooking Activity: Make Your Own Butter

Collect small baby food jars, fill them halfway with heavy cream (also called whipping cream), then shake and roll them until the butter thickens. You can sing this fun song while the children are shaking their jars.
[15 min.]

Making Butter Boogie

(Tune of "Twinkle, Twinkle")

Shake it up
Shake it down
Shake it, shake it all around.

Shake it high
Shake it low
Shake it, shake it to and fro.

Shake it over
Shake it under
Pretty soon, you'll have butter!

I bring in my bread machine and bake bread the same day we make butter. Measuring ingredients is a good math lesson and a great hands-on activity for the kids. Borrow extra bread machines if you can.

✪ Additional Activity: Dancing Ducks

Cut duck shapes from yellow construction paper. Let the children color the eyes and beaks. Cut large rubber bands in half and tape the pieces on the back of the duck shapes. The rubber bands are the duck's legs. Cut duck feet from orange paper and tape one to each rubber band leg.

dancing duck

Additional Resources to Share

Books

Brown, Ruth. *The Big Sneeze*. One afternoon a farmer dozes in the barn. A fly lands on his nose and his resulting sneeze sets off a chain of events.

Lacome, Julie. *I'm a Jolly Farmer*. Candlewick, 1994. An adorable girl and her dog frolic on a farm.

Lodge, Jo. *Busy Farm: A Counting Book*. Dial, 1999. A pop-up, pull-tab book with kittens hiding, goats eating clothes, and pigs splashing.

Cassette

Thompson, Kim Mitzo. *Farm Animals*. Twin Sisters Productions, 1999. Original songs about farm animals and being a farmer.

Video

The Midnight Farm. Weston Woods. 5 min. A gentle story of a child who awakens and explores a sleeping farm. From the book by Reeve Lindbergh.

CD-ROM

Come to the Playroom. Entertainment Technology. Click on the ABC book and select the farm scene. Letters of the alphabet are displayed on the top of the scene. When clicked on, objects beginning with those letters will appear and be spoken. They can be placed into the farm scene. [school games]

Farm Animals for Windows. Wierenga Software. Create a farm story, then color and print. [printing software]

Let's Explore the Farm. TDC Software. Features animals and machines common to a farm. Milk a cow, visit the chicken coop, harvest corn, and see a beaver dam. [factual information, activities]

Internet Sites

Michigan Department of Agriculture: Kids Korner
www.mda.state.mi.us/kids/index.html
Check out the county fair, read farm life stories, or look at pictures of kids involved in agricultural activities.

Owl Educational Software
www.yourchildlearns.com/farm.htm
Download "Make a Farm." Print of farm animals, fences, and buildings to make a paper farm.

Red Bluff Ranch: Kid's Farm
www.kidsfarm.com/wheredo.htm
Information on animals, equipment, crops and more.

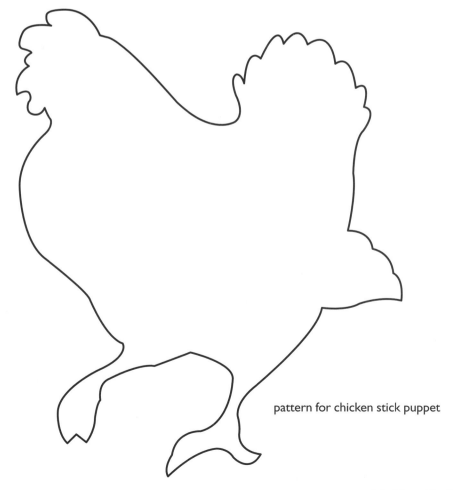

pattern for chicken stick puppet

Flies

Setting the Scene: Fly Facts

Just thinking about flies unnerves some people! But kids will love meeting these critters up close. Start off by listing the yucky things that flies do. Use the book *Yuck: Big Book of Little Horrors* by Robert Snedden. (Simon & Schuster, 1996) to zoom in on flies.
[3 min.]

Internet Site: There Was an Old Lady Who Swallowed a Fly

www.EnchantedLearning.com/rhymes/ladyfly/

This website features a rebus version of this folk song. Site by Enchanted Learning Software.
[3 min.]

Book: *Old Black Fly*

A rhyming alphabet book about the fate of a bothersome fly. Jim Aylesworth. Holt, 1992.
[5 min.]

Five Flies

Five black flies, buzzing through a hive,
(hold up five fingers)
One snuck some honey, then took a deep dive.
("tiptoe" fingers)

Four black flies, buzzing by the door,
(hold up four fingers)
One flew in and was no more.
(put one finger down)

Three black flies, buzzing in the trees,
(hold up three fingers)
One landed on a horses knee.
(point to knee)

Two black flies, buzzing through a shoe,
(hold up two fingers)
One held his nose and said, "Pee-yoo!"
(hold nose)

One black fly, landed on a bun.
(hold up one finger)
"Splat," goes the fly swatter—*(clap)*
Now there are none.
[Fingerplay—1 min.]

Book: *You Can't Catch Me*

A pesky fly bothers every single animal it meets except for the turtle. By Joanne Oppenheim. Houghton Mifflin, 1998.
[6 min.]

Creepy Crawly

A fly went creepy crawly,
(stand and creep hands up from toes)
Climbing up the wall-y.
The weather became squally.
(hold up arms and sway like a tree in the wind)
And rain began to fall-y.
(flutter fingers down like rain)
Down from the wall-y
Fell the creepy crawly.
Flump!
(fall to the ground)
[Action Rhyme—1 min.]

Craft: Fly Puppet

Use the fly pattern on page 45. Copy onto stiff paper, color and cut out. Attach to craft sticks to create pesky fly puppets.
[5 min.]

Video: *I Know an Old Lady*

Weston Woods. From the book by Nancy Willard. Cumulative tale of an old woman who eats all different kinds of creatures with humorous results.
[8 min.]

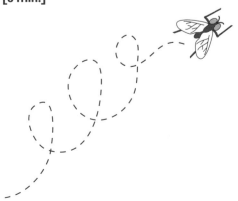

Additional Resources to Share

Books

McClintock, Marshall. *A Fly Went By*. Random House, 1987. The classic rhymed tale of the chaos that happens as a result of a fly.

Wilkinson, Valerie. *Flies Are Fascinating*. Children's Press, 1994. A must have for any child learning about insects, their habits, and body structures.

CD-ROM

Biolab: Fly. Pierian Springs Software. Watch the science lab animation about fruit flies. [factual information, activities]

New Frog and Fly. Bill Lyn/Simtech Publications. Help the frog capture flies and be rewarded with "burps." [game for very young children]

Internet Sites

@dver@ctive: Lickety-Splat! Eat flies!
http://207.69.132.225/neatstuf/frog/frog.htm
A free downloadable children's game about a frog and flies. Requires Shockwave.

Emmett Scott's Cartoon Corner: Help Peetie Count the Flies
www.cartooncorner.com/puzzlefolder/countdaflies/counttheflys.html
A child's game featuring flies and bees.

Enchanted Learning Software: "Fiddle Dee Dee"
www.EnchantedLearning.com/rhymes/Flybee.shtml
This is a rebus version of the popular rhyme about a fly that married a bumblebee.

pattern for fly puppet

Friends from Around the World

Activity: Friends from Around the World Crown

Cut heavy paper into a 1" strip that will fit around your head. Using the pattern on page 47, cut out seven child shapes. Decorate each shape to represent a different country's ethnic dress and facial features. Arrange the child shapes on the paper strip and tape them down. Staple the strip to fit around your head and wear the crown for your storytime.
[7–10 min.]

CD-ROM: *Let's Be Friends*

Six children from Poland, China, Italy, Sri Lanka, El Salvador and Iran tell about their cultures using photos and narration. Nectar Foundation. [factual information]
[4 min. for one county]

Book: *For Every Child, A Better World*

This book shows the stark contrast in living, eating, and health conditions for children around the world, offering hope that the problems can be solved. By Louise Gikow. Golden, 1993.
[5 min.]

The More We Get Together

(Tune of "Have You Ever Seen a Lassie")

The more we get together
Together, together,
The more we get together
The happier we'll be.

For your friends are my friends
And my friends are your friends,
The more we get together
The happier we'll be.
[Song—1 min.]

Ten Little Friends

I have ten little friends
And they all belong to me. *(hold up ten fingers)*

We like to do things
Would you like to see?

We can hug tight *(make a fist)*
Run away. *(make fingers "run")*
Or play hide and seek all day. *(put hands behind back)*

We can jump rope high *(put hands over head)*
Or play hopscotch low *(put hands down low)*
We can sit down quiet and rest just so. *(put hands in lap)*
[Fingerplay—1 min.]

I Met a Friend

(Tune of "The Farmer in the Dell")

I met a friend,
I met a friend,
When I came to the library today,
I met a friend.

The friend's name is _____.
The friend's name is _____.
When I came to the library today,
The friend's name is _____.
(Insert the names of the children present)
[Song—1 min.]

Internet Site: Tots TV Tilly, Tom & Tiny Puppets

www.pbs.org/totstv/english/patterns.html

Print a friend puppet by clicking on the one you would like and following directions. Site from the Public Broadcasting System.
[9 min.]

Video: *All the Colors of the Earth*

Weston Woods. From the book by Sheila Hamanaka. This rhyming multicultural tale beautifully describes diversity in children around the world.
[7 min.]

✪ Additional Activity: Famous Buildings

Use Duplo or Lego building blocks to try and create famous structures from around the world, such as: France—The Eiffel Tower; India—Taj Mahal; Japan—A Pagoda; England—London Bridge.

✪ Additional Activity: Friendship Mini-book

Make a four-page, heart-shaped mini book. Staple the pages together. On each page, draw pictures of things you do with a friend and caption them.

Additional Resources to Share

Books

Agell, Charlotte. *Dancing Feet*. Gulliver, 1994. A group of multicultural kids show various parts of their bodies and what they do with them.

Baer, Edith. *This Is the Way We Go to School*. Scholastic, 1990. Children the world over are shown using various modes of transportation to get to school.

Leventhal, Debra. *What Is Your Language?* Dutton, 1994. Emphasizes the many languages spoken throughout the world.

CD-ROM

Alpha Betty and Friends. Micrograms Software. Play a simple letter game with Betty and her friends. [games]

Four Footed Friends. T/Maker Company. Ten screens allow multi-language exploration of animals and other icons. [factual information]

Playground of Friends. Comfy. Press the keys to learn about sharing, friendship, taking turns, cooperation, manners and more. [activities]

Internet Sites

Bando Elementary School: Symphony of Friendship
www.mandala.co.jp/B9/P00E.html
This online story is about how the Japanese custom of playing Beethoven's Ninth Symphony at Christmas first started. Written and illustrated by school children from Bando, Japan.

Hoot and Kat "Best Friends"
www.abctooncenter.com/hkbestx.htm
A children's read-a-long story about friendship. Site by Jack Armstrong.

pattern for "Friends from Around the World" crown

Frogs

Setting the Scene: Fun with Frogs

Wear green the day you do your frog storytime. Have a bowl of raisins and pretend they are flies. Tell the kids you like frogs so much that you have decided to try and eat flies the way they do. Use the pattern on page 49 to make frog nametags or enlarge to use as a coloring sheet.
[3 min.]

CD-ROM: *Frog and Toad Are Friends*

Play one of the stories involving the humorous antics of friendly Frog and his buddy Toad. Foxtoons Interactive. [interactive stories]
[3 min.]

Five Frisky Frogs

(Hold up five fingers and bend one down for each verse)

Five frisky frogs, hopping along the shore.
One hopped into the pond– *Splash!* –
and then there were four.

Four frisky frogs, climb up a tree.
One fell in the grass – *Boom!* –
and then there were three.

Three frisky frogs bathing in the dew,
One caught a cold – *Ahchoo!* –
and then there were two.

Two frisky frogs sleeping in the sun,
One slept the day away – *Snore!* –
So then there was just one.

One frisky frog sitting on a stone,
Let's call his friends back – *Yoo hoo!* –
so he won't be alone.
[Fingerplay—I min.]

Book: *Jump, Frog, Jump!*

A cumulative tale in which a frog tries to catch a fly while evading his own captors. Robert Kalan. Greenwillow, 1981.
[4 min.]

Internet Site: BZZZ!

www.astraware.com/pc/bzzz

Download this free game to help a frog catch flies with his tongue. Site by Astrosoft.
[5 min.]

Baby Frogs

"Ribbit, ribbit," said mama frog
While sitting on a brown muddy log.
"Where are my babies, where can they be?"
Then out of the pond jumped one, two, three.
(hold up fingers one at a time)

She was happy, but where were the others?
She couldn't see.
So "Ribbit, ribbit" she called again,
And out jumped four, five, six, seven, eight, nine, ten.
(hold up remaining fingers)
[Fingerplay—I min.]

Book: *The Frog Alphabet Book*

This book shows frogs and other amphibians, one for each letter of the alphabet. By Jerry Pallotta. Charlesbridge, 1990.
[6 min.]

Video: *A Boy, a Dog, and a Frog*

Weston Woods. From the book by Mercer Mayer. Adventures of a boy and his dog who chase after an uncooperative frog.
[9 min.]

✪ Additional Activity: Five Frisky Frogs

Make a log by putting a man's brown sock on your arm. Make frogs out of green pom-poms with wiggly eyes glued on. Attach Velcro to the bottom of the pom-poms. Do the "Baby Frogs" rhyme above, and remove each frog.

Additional Resources to Share

Books

London, Jonathan. *Froggy Gets Dressed*. Viking, 1992. Froggy is repeatedly called back inside the house by his mother, who requires him to put on more and more winter clothes.

Thayer, Mike. *In the Middle of the Puddle*. Harper and Row, 1988. A frog and a turtle watch as first the rain and then the sun transform their puddle.

Cassette

Grosvenor, Terry. *Fun Songs for Tadpoles to Frogs*. Grosvenor, 1994.

CD-ROM

Melno the Frog: A Musical Fairy Tale. Windy Hill. Listen and watch the musical cartoon about Melno. [music, story]

Tomorrow's Promise Spelling. Josten's Learning. Click on the pond. Spell simple words and help the frog earn flies. [spelling activities]

Internet Sites

The Froggy Page
www.frog.simplenet.com/froggy
All kinds of frog information, from the scientific to the silly. Contains music, sounds, stories, pictures and more. Site by Sandra Loosemore.

Slimy Frog Software: Koji the Frog
www.electricgames.com/mac-games/k/
mac-kojithefrog.html
Download the game for the Macintosh and avoid snakes, gophers, and bees while eating bugs.

pattern for frog nametag or coloring sheet

Go Batty

Setting the Scene: Create a Bat Cave

Use a large cardboard box or drape a dark sheet over a table. Decorate the inside with paper bats hung from strings taped to the top of the cave. Provide a flashlight for the children to shine in the cave and see the bats.

Use the pattern on page 51 to make a bat nametag or coloring sheet as the children enter the room.
[5 min.]

Book: *Stellaluna*

This is the popular story of the baby bat who is separated from her mother and tries to live as a baby bird. By Janell Cannon. Harcourt Brace, 1993.
[9 min.]

I'm a Little Batlet

(Tune of "I'm a Little Teapot")

I'm a little batlet, small and shy,
Hanging in a tree so near to the sky.
When the night is starting
And the bugs come out—
Watch me and the other bats fly right out!
[Song—1 min.]

CD-ROM: *Sesame Street Numbers*

Move the blinking star over to the Count's castle and click on it. Explore the castle and find and count the bats hiding there. [educational games]
[4 min]

Five Brown Bats

(hold fist facing down and extend one finger down for each bat)

Five brown bats hanging upside down,
The first one did not make a sound.
The second one said, "I'll fly far tonight."
The third one said, "But not in sunlight."
The fourth one said, "Let's go get some flies."

The fifth one said, "In the dark skies."
Five brown bats hanging upside down,
Asleep in a cave with their wings wrapped around.
[Fingerplay—1 min.]

Five Little Bats

(Use the rhythm and motions of "Five Little Ducks")

Five little bats went flying one day,
Away in the dark and far away.
Mother bat said, "*Flap, flap, flap.*"
And four little bats came flying back.
(Repeat with 4, 3, 2, 1 and none)

Then mother bat said, "*Flap, flap, flap!*"
And five little bats came flying back.
[Action Rhyme—1 min.]

Internet Site: Bat Flip Book

www.cccoe.k12.ca.us/bats/flip.html

Make a bat flying flip book to print, color and staple. Site by Contra Costa County Office of Education.
[9 min.]

✪ Additional Activity: Batty Puppet

Enlarge and copy the bat pattern below onto black construction paper. Color in the features with chalk. Cut slits on the two lines. Push a craft stick through the slits to make a puppet.

pattern for batty puppet

Additional Resources to Share

Books

Cannon, Annie. *The Bat in the Boot*. Orchard, 1996. Based on a true incident, this is the story of a baby bat found by two children in their father's boot.

Cooper, Ann C. *Bats: Swift Shadows in the Twilight*. Roberts Rinehart, 1994. Published in cooperation with the Denver Museum of Natural History, this beautifully illustrated book uses an enlightening blend of folktales and facts to show readers the true nature of this mild-mannered friend to humans—the bat. Includes fun and easy craft ideas and covers over 1,000 species of bats.

Krulik, Nancy. *The Magic School Bus Going Batty: A Book about Bats*. Scholastic, 1996. When the Magic School Bus turns into a bat, the gang gets the inside story on this eerie yet fascinating creature of the night.

CD-ROM

Ozzie's World. Knowledge Arts. Go to the forest to camp, and click on the bat. Listen to the bat facts and bat fictions. [factual information, activities]

Stellaluna. Living Books. An animated version of the story, with songs and a bat quiz. [story, music, activities]

Video

The Magic School Bus Goes Batty. PBS. 30 min. Ms. Frizzle and her class discover how bats survive, hunt bugs and use echolocation.

Internet Sites

Bat Conservation International: New Bat Facts
www.batcon.org
Go to this site for bat photos and facts.

Enchanted Learning Software: Egg Carton Animals
www.enchantedlearning.com/crafts/Eggcarton.shtml
Provides instructions on how to make a bat from an egg carton.

pattern for bat nametag or coloring sheet

Hedgehogs

Setting the Scene: Nocturnal Animals

Hedgehogs are nocturnal animals. Explain to the children that this means they are up and playing while we sleep. Darken the room and challenge the children to attempt to locate an object in the dark. Was it hard? Talk about the other senses that hedgehogs use to find their way around, such as an excellent sense of smell.
[6 min.]

Book: *The Hat*

The story of a hedgehog who gets a sock stuck on his head and convinces all the other animals that it is a fashionable hat. By Jan Brett. Putnam, 1997.
[7 min.]

Hedgehog in His Hole

A hedgehog lived in a little hole,
(hold up fist with thumb tucked inside)
Lived so quietly in his hole.
When all was quiet as can be ...
Out popped he!
(pop up thumb)
[Action Rhyme—1 min.]

CD-ROM: *Zoo-opolis*

Take the interactive zoo tour to the mammals section and choose hedgehogs. Soleil Software. [factual information, movies, games, puzzles]
[7 min.]

Hedgehog, Hedgehog

Hedgehog, hedgehog,
Rolled up in a ball.
Hedgehog, hedgehog,
Won't wake up at all.

Hedgehog, hedgehog,
What a funny sight.
Hedgehog, hedgehog,
Won't wake up 'till night.
[Chant—1 min.]

Book: *The Prickly Hedgehog*

A young hedgehog is separated from his family and suffers a series of spine-related mishaps. By Mark Ezra. Interlink, 1996.
[6 min.]

Internet Site: 12 Hedgehogs Puzzle Game

http://fohnix.metronet.com/~mcgary/12hogs.html

Pick a hedgehog and try and beat the computer in the logic puzzle.
[5 min.]

Internet Site: Hedgehog movie

http://homearts.com:80/depts/pastime/hedgehb8.htm

View this video of a hedgehog in MPEG or QuickTime formats.
[5 min.]

✪ Additional Activity: Toothpick Hedgehog

Copy the pattern on page 53 for each child. Give them a supply of toothpicks and glue. Let them create spines on the hedgehog by gluing on toothpicks.

Additional Resources to Share

Books

Crozat, Frances. *I Am a Little Hedgehog*. Barron's, 1996. A mix of fact and fiction describes the life of a young hedgehog.

Waddell, Martin. *The Happy Hedgehog Band*. Candlewick, 1992. A group of merry hedgehogs create their own special band.

CD-ROM

My Neighborhood. Edmark. Get on the bus and go to the pet store. Find and play the puzzle about the hedgehog. [stories, games]

Once Upon a Forest. Sanctuary Woods. Listen to the sound effects and music in this story of a mouse, mole, and hedgehog. [stories]

Internet Sites

Hedgehog Review: All About Hedgehogs
www.hedgehog-review.com/CR/hedge.html
Links to other sites on hedgehogs, and lots of information on hedgehog lifestyles, care and feeding.

Hedgehogs.net
www.hedgehogs.net/
Good website that offers information about hedgehogs as pets, care and feeding, with many illustrations.

Rene Romeg's African Pigmy Hedgehog Page
www.sunflower.org/~ronromig/index.htm
Features photos, and pros and cons of keeping a hedgehog as a pet.

pattern for toothpick hedgehog

How Does Your Garden Grow?

Activity: Planting Seeds

Purchase several packets of different kinds of seeds. Read the directions on the packages to the children. Allow them to select seeds to plant in paper cups pre-filled with soil. Children can just poke a finger in the soil, drop in a seed and cover. Provide moist towelettes to clean hands. After planting, sing the following song.
[8 min.]

Little Seed

(Tune of "I'm a Little Teapot")

Here's a little seed in the dark, dark ground.
Out comes the warm sun, yellow and round.
Down comes the rain, wet and slow.
Up comes the little seed, grow, grow, grow!
[Song—4 min.]

Book: *The Surprise Garden*

Brief first-person text describes what kids do with a variety of seeds in a garden. By Zoe Hall. Scholastic, 1998.
[6 min.]

Five Little Sunflowers

Five little sunflowers stand in the sun.
(hold up five fingers)
See their heads nodding, bowing one by one.
(bend fingers)
Then down, down, down, comes the gentle rain.
(wiggle fingers down as rain)
And the five little flowers lift their heads again.
(hold up five fingers)
[Fingerplay—1 min.]

Internet Site: One Seed Can Make a Difference

www.kidscount.com/jack/read.html

This is an online story about gardening. Site by Kids Count Entertainment.
[5 min.]

My Garden

This is my garden, *(hold one hand out palm up)*
I'll rake it with care. *(rake fingers across palm)*
And then some flower seeds, *(sprinkle seeds)*
I will plant there. *(pat palm)*

The sun will shine, *(circle arms overhead)*
And the rain will fall, *(wiggle fingers down)*
And my garden will blossom, *(make fists and open slowly)*
To grow straight and tall. *(stretch arms over head)*
[Action Rhyme—1 min.]

Craft: Garden Pockets

For each pocket, you will need 1½, 6" paper plates. Color the half plate as grass and the whole plate as sky. Punch eight holes around the edge of both plates and use yarn to lace them together. Cut pictures of plants and flowers from magazines or make paper flowers to tuck in the grass pocket.
[10 min.]

garden pocket

Additional Resources to Share

Books

Bunting, Eve. *Flower Garden*. Harcourt Brace, 1994. An urban child and her father buy plants, soil, and a window box to make a surprise for her mother.

Hines, Anna. *Miss Emma's Wild Garden*. Greenwillow, 1997. Young Chloe notices that Miss Emma's garden grows wild and unruly, not like her father's neat organized garden.

Stevens, Janet. *Tops and Bottoms*. Harcourt Brace, 1995. A folktale in which a lazy bear is tricked by gardening rabbits.

Video

Titch. Weston Woods. 4 min. From the book by Pat Hutchins. Titch feels left out because he is so much smaller than his siblings, until he gets a tiny seed that grows into a flower much bigger than anything they have.

CD-ROM

Forever Growing Garden. Sierra Online. Children can create a fantasy garden using this CD. The program simulates the planting of seeds, watering, and a tour of animated plants. Flowers can also be made into an arrangement by visiting the florist shop. [activities]

Mr. Potato Head Saves Veggie Valley. Playschool Software/ Hasbro Interactive. Help Mr. Potato Head and his daughter Sweet Potato lure a storm cloud to Veggie Valley in order to save the garden. [stories, activities]

Ozzie's Funtime Garden. Digital Impact. Click on the plants and sunflowers in the garden. [science]

Internet Sites

Kids Valley Garden
www.arnprior.com/kidsgarden/index.htm
Information for kids on planning and planting a garden. Site by Louise Larabie.

I Love Sunflowers
www.sunflowergal.com/sunflows/sunflow.htm
This site contains photos of sunflowers, links to other sunflower sites, poems and more. Site by Dawn Banks George.

Planet Zoom: Vegetable Head Game
www.planetzoom.com/VegetableHead/vegetableHead.htm
Kids can make faces on different vegetables.

Human Body

Setting the Scene: Obstacle Course

Set up a mini-obstacle course with jumping jacks, jogging in place, crawling under a chair, and a beanbag throw. Let the kids try it as they enter the story area. Talk with the kids about the different body parts they used to complete each item of the course.
[5 min.]

Book: *I Know Where My Food Goes*

Sam tells the whole soupy, gloopy story of digestion. From the Sam's Science series. By Jacqui Maynard. Candlewick, 1999.
[4 min.]

Internet Site: Human Anatomy Online

www.innerbody.com/htm/body.html

Graphic illustrations of the human skeletal and other systems in our bodies. Site by Inner Learning Online.
[6 min.]

Pointy Fingers

Two pointy fingers I can show,
(hold up two fingers)
Way up high or way down low.
(move fingers high and low)
With my right, I point to my toe,
(point at toe)
With my left, I point where to go.
(point left)
With both fingers, I point at my knee,
(point to knee)
My fingers are so helpful to me!
[Action Rhyme—1 min.]

CD-ROM: *My Amazing Human Body*

Play "Take Me Apart" and put Seemore Skeleton back together correctly. Dorling Kindersley Multimedia.
[factual information, activities]
[7 min.]

Hands

This is my right hand
I raise it up high.
(raise up right hand)

This is my left hand
I raise to the sky.
(raise up left hand)

Right hand *(show palm)*
Left hand *(show palm)*
Roll them around.
(roll hands)

Left hand *(show palm)*
Right hand *(show palm)*
Pound, pound, pound.
(pound one palm with the other)
[Action Rhyme—1 min.]

Craft: Body Model

Materials for each child:

• brown paper grocery sack
• tagboard circle
• one small red balloon
• straws cut into sections
• two pink oval sponges
• brown yarn

Cut off the bottom of the sack and then cut down one side to open up the bag. The sack serves as the body, which stands up like a display board. The other materials are applied as follows: The tagboard circle is the head; the red balloon (slightly inflated) is the heart; the straw sections are strung on the yarn as the spine; and the rest of the yarn makes the intestines. The two oval sponges serve as the lungs.
[10 min.]

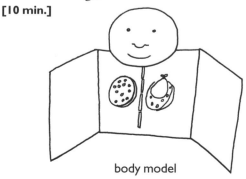

body model

Additional Resources to Share

Books

Boynton, Sandra. *Horns to Toes and in Between*. Simon & Schuster, 1984. A rhyming book with comical creatures who describe their body parts.

Kates, Bobbi. *We're Different, We're the Same*. Random House, 1992. The illustrations in this book show the similarities and differences in body parts of both humans and puppets.

Martin, Bill, and John Archambault. *Here Are My Hands*. Henry Holt, 1987. Multicultural children show hands and other body parts in this rhymed tale.

Video

The Magic School Bus: Inside Ralphie. PBS. 30 min. When Ralphie gets a cold and can't host the Frizzle News Network, Ms. Frizzle and the gang travel through his bloodstream and learn how the human body fights germs.

Cassette

So Big by Hap Palmer. Hap-Pal Music, 1994. Activity songs that tap a child's desire to sing, move and make believe. Body songs include "I'm a Pretzel," "Put Your Hands in the Air," Growing," and "Ten Wiggle Worms."

CD-ROM

Welcome to Bodyland. TimeLife IVI. Listen to the answers to questions about the body from Rikki and Hiccup the parrot. [factual information]

What Is a Bellybutton? TimeLife IVI. Baxter the bear reads a story about bellybuttons after visiting a doctor's office. [factual information in story form]

Internet Sites

Franklin Institute: Heart Preview Gallery
http://sln2.fi.edu/biosci/preview/heartpreview.html
Take a virtual tour through a human heart.

GE Research and Development: Three Dimensional Medical Reconstruction
www.crd.ge.com/esl/cgsp/projects/medical
These amazing movies in MPG format take you through various organs and body parts. Click on any of the fly-through movies to download and play.

Kidshealth.org: How the Body Works
http://kidshealth.org/parent/healthy/bodyworks.html
Provides an animated look at the human respiratory, circulation, digestive and other related systems. Macromedia Shockwave is needed. Site sponsored by the Nemours Foundation.

Jobs

Setting the Scene: Talk About Jobs

Using a chalkboard or large pad and marker, compile a list of the occupations or jobs held by the parents or guardians of the children in your group. Brainstorm some additional careers and add them to the list. Bring in some hats associated with occupations, such as a baker's hat, fireman's hat, etc., and record the guesses the children make as you model the hats.
[6 min.]

Book: *I Am Me!*

Nine children imagine their future careers based on activities they enjoy today. By Alexa Brandenberg. Harcourt Brace, 1996.
[5 min.]

Workers

This worker feeds the animals at the zoo,
This worker makes a sole for a shoe.
This worker drives an engine to a fire,
This worker mends a high electric wire.
This worker drives a sweeper through the street,
This worker sells some food for me to eat.
This worker helps the swimmers in the sun,
And they are all good workers, every one.
[Rhyme—I min.]

Internet Site: Presto

www.mamamedia.com/home/my_mamamedia/home.html

Click on the "Surprise" button and then on "Presto" to build your own town. Site by MaMaMedia.com
[7 min.]

If I Were…

If I were a baker, what would I do?
Bake lots of cookies for me and you.
(make circles with thumb and forefinger)

If I were a veterinarian, what would I do?
Care for a pet that is special to you.
(pretend to pet an animal)

If I were a dentist, what would I do?
I would clean your teeth for you.
(pretend to brush teeth)
[Fingerplay—I min.]

CD-ROM: *Adventures with Oslo: Tools and Gadgets*

Go to "Donna's Dilemma" and help Donna decide which simple machine to use. Science for Kids. [stories, poems, games]
[9 min.]

Five Fun Hats

In my box are five fun hats.
The first one is a nurse's cap.
The second one is red for a fire fighter.
The third one, a baker's, is tall and lighter.
Wear the fourth one for baseball.
Take along your bat.
Save the fifth one for your birthday.
It's a party hat!
[Rhyme—I min.]

Additional Resources to Share

Books

Galdone, Paul. *Little Red Hen*. Seabury, 1973. The traditional tale of the hen who does all the work and reaps all the rewards.

Paulsen, Gary. *Worksong*. Harcourt Brace, 1997. People at work doing their jobs are lyrically depicted and illustrated.

Radford, Derek. *Building Machines and What They Do*. Candlewick, 1992. A factual book about machinery related to several aspects of construction.

Video

The Little Red Hen. Weston Woods. 11 min. Traditional story of the industrious hen who does all the work and reaps all the rewards.

CD-ROM

The Busy People of Hamsterland. Fisher Price. This story about a village of industrious people teaches about a variety of professions. [story]

Kids on Site. Digital Pictures. Drive an excavator, bulldozer, steamroller, or wrecking ball at a construction site. [factual information, activities]

Richard Scarry's How Things Work in Busytown. Paramount Interactive. Children learn about different jobs at places throughout Busytown, such as a working in the bakery, driving a garbage truck, working at the recycling plant or assembly plant, and more. [factual information, activities]

Internet Sites

Dental Website
www.smiledoc.com/dentist/quicktim.html
At this site, from Drs. Kim Loos and R. K. Boyden, you can download free dental software for children, as well as a virtual reality rotating tooth.

Fisher Price: Games and Activities
www.fisher-price.com/us/fun/default.asp
Select the "Who's at the Door?" game and listen to the dog for directions. Select the Little People that match what the dog says. Or, select the "Rescue Heroes" comic and help the fire fighters and other emergency personnel do their jobs.

Kids & Careers Website
www.bcit.tec.nj.us/childcareer/Default.htm
This website provides resources for career exploration with children. Includes games, an on-line manual, and related links.

Places for Kids Online
www.geocities.com/Heartland/Ranch/3107/kids.html
A score of good children's games and puzzles.

The Jungle

Setting the Scene: Explore the Jungle

A jungle is a tropical forest or woodland. Share stories to make the children aware of some of the animals and plants that are found there. Pretend to pack a backpack with water, food, and first aid kit so that you and the children can take an imaginary hike through the jungle. Don't forget to take your camera! Pretend to take photographs of animals you might see on your hike. Use a jungle sound effects tape in the background.
[5 min.]

Book: *The Rain Forest Counts!*

Introduces rain forest animals while counting from one to ten and back down again. By Lisa McCourt. Bridgewater, 1997.
[5 min.]

Twelve Animals in the Jungle

(Tune of "The Twelve Days of Christmas")

One day in the jungle, what did I see?
A monkey in a banana tree.

(Repeat as if singing the "Twelve Days of Christmas" using the following verses.)

Two flying squirrels
Three butterflies
Four boa constrictors
Five brown tarantulas
Six sloths a-sleeping
Seven piranha swimming
Eight toucans squawking
Nine frogs a -hopping
Ten lions sleeping
Eleven hummingbirds humming
Twelve crocodiles snapping
[Song—1 min.]

Internet Site: Adopt a Rainforest Animal

www.kidsdomain.com/holiday/earthday/adopt.html

Adopt these "virtual rainforest pets." Animals are animated gifs for your computer which come complete with adoption certificates. Site by Kid's Domain/Soleil Software.
[6 min.]

A Walk in the Jungle

Giraffes are tall, with necks so long.
(stand on toes and raise arms up high)
Elephants' trunks are strong.
(hand arm in front of nose like a trunk)
Zebras have stripes of black and white.
(act as if painting stripes on self)
Bats are awake all through the night.
(make bat with hands)
Alligators swim in pools so deep.
(make alligator mouth with arms)
On the trunks of trees tarantulas creep.
(make spider creep with hand)
[Action Rhyme—1 min.]

CD-ROM: *Zurk's Rainforest Lab*

When you see the animals who appear randomly on the jungle screen, click on them to have facts read aloud to the children. Soliel Software.
[7min.]

Video: *Brian Wildsmith's Wild Animals*

Weston Woods. From the book by Brian Wildsmith.
[6 min.]

✪ Additional Activity: Paper Bromeliad

A bromeliad is a type of plant that grows in the jungle or rainforest, usually attached to the trunk of a tree. To make a paper bromeliad, you will need a 10 oz. plastic cup, green and red construction paper, scissors, glue and crayons.

Using the patterns on page 61, enlarge the patterns by 20%. Trace pattern A onto red paper and cut out. Trace pattern B onto green paper and cut out. Wrap the red paper around the cup and glue into place as shown in the illustration below. Wrap the green paper around the outside of the red paper and glue into place. Curl the leaves downward to create a bromeliad.

 red green

Additional Resources to Share

Books

Hindley, Judy. *Into the Jungle*. Candlewick, 1994. A brother and sister venture where tigers lurk.

Staines, Bill. *All God's Critters Got a Place in the Choir*. Puffin, 1993. The lyrics to folk musician Bill Staines' rollicking song "All God's Critters Got a Place in the Choir" finds everyone from the fiddling cricket to the hollering hoot owl "clapping their hands, or paws, or anything they got." A fun-filled, full-color picture book kids will love!

West, Colin. *One Day in the Jungle*. Candlewick, 1997. A cumulative tale of "achoos" and "bless yous" in a jungle setting.

CD-ROM

Destination Rainforest. Edmark. Go to a Panamanian Rainforest and use "stickers" to create your own interactive story. Save the story and the program will read it back to you. [factual information, activities]

Let's Explore the Jungle. GT Interactive. Learn about the jungles of Asia, Africa, and the Amazon. Buzzy the Bug guides the child through 30 locations with more than 210 objects and five educational games. [factual information, games]

Internet Sites:

Rainforest Action Network: The Rainforest
www.ran.org/ran/kids_action/index.html
This site contains information on the animals and native peoples of the rainforest, a question and answer section, tips on how children can help save the rainforest, a kid's art gallery, and more.

Rainforest Alliance: For Kids and Teachers
www.rainforest-alliance.org/kids&teachers/index.html
This site offers a wide array of information and activities on the rainforest for children and teachers. Includes a tropical coloring book, rainforest stories, the School of Amazon Painting, frog pond resources and more.

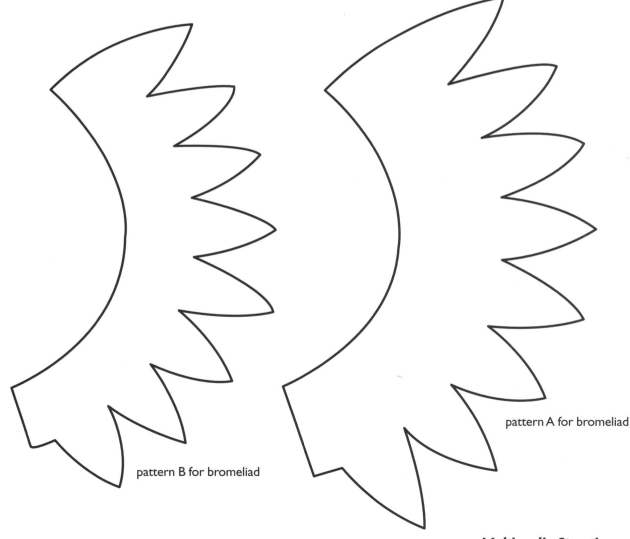

pattern B for bromeliad

pattern A for bromeliad

Lovely Lizards

Activity: Play Hide and Seek Lizard

Stuff an old green sock, tie off the end and decorate with markers. Add a tail and legs by twisting pipe cleaners around the sock. While the children close their eyes, hide the lizard in the story area. Have a little of the lizard showing for the youngsters to find it easily. The person who finds the lizard gets to hide it the next time. This game can lead to a discussion of how chameleons use camouflage to hide in their natural homes.

[5 min.]

Book: *A Color of His Own*

A young chameleon is unsatisfied changing colors all the time until he meets another chameleon to befriend. Leo Lionni. Turtleback, 1997.

[6 min.]

Did You Ever See a Lizard?

(Tune of "Did You Ever See a Lassie?")

Did you ever see a lizard, a lizard, a lizard,
Did you ever see a lizard, all scaly and green?
With yellow eyes and a green nose,
And a long tail and sharp toes.
Did you ever see a lizard, all scaly and green.

[Song—1 min.]

CD-ROM: *My First Incredible Amazing Dictionary*

Click on the letter "C," then choose the icon for the chameleon. Click on the lizard photo and watch it change colors. DK Multimedia. [reference]

[3 min.]

Book: *The Yucky Reptile Alphabet Book*

Beautiful paintings illustrate exotic, interesting reptiles. By Jerry Pallotta. Charlesbridge, 1990.

[7 min.]

Five Green Lizards

One green lizard, sleeping all alone.
Two green lizards, sitting on a stone.
Three green lizards, running up a tree.
Four green lizards, as still as can be.
Five green lizards, looking at me.

[Fingerplay—1 min.]

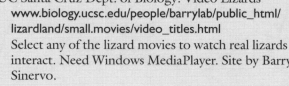

Internet Site: IguanaCam

http://iguana.images.com

Watch the iguanas on this live Webcam. Site from Iguana Images.

[5 min.]

Additional Resources to Share

Books

Jenkins, Mark. *Chameleons Are Cool*. Candlewick, 1998. A factual book by a biologist that tells fun and interesting facts about chameleons.

Smith, Trevor. *Amazing Lizards*. Knopf, 1990. The authors use dramatic examples of each species to introduce readers to basic facts about frogs, toads, and lizards. The text is disjointed, but exciting, and the photographs are brilliant.

Video

"The Mixed-Up Chameleon" from *The Very Hungry Caterpillar and Other Stories*. Walt Disney Home Video, 1993.

CD-ROM

Eyewitness Children's Encyclopedia. Dorling Kindersley Multimedia. Click on the letter "L" and go to lizard. Explore the pictures and activities. [factual information]

Encyclopedia of U.S. Endangered Species. Softkey International. Pick one of the species of lizards from the index. After choosing a lizard, choose the large picture to show the children what it looks like. [factual information]

Internet Sites

Lizard! Lizards! Lizards!
www.sirius.com/~jwebster/Lizards/LizardsLizardsLizards.html
Lizard games, books, pictures, links, and more. Site by Jim Webster.

UC Santa Cruz Dept. of Biology: Video Lizards
www.biology.ucsc.edu/people/barrylab/public_html/lizardland/small.movies/video_titles.html
Select any of the lizard movies to watch real lizards interact. Need Windows MediaPlayer. Site by Barry Sinervo.

Lucky Leprechauns

Game: Run, Little Leprechaun

Have the children sit in a circle. Play Irish music as the children pass around a shamrock made out of construction paper. When the music stops, the child holding the shamrock stops passing. All the children yell "Run Little Leprechaun!" The child with the shamrock gets up and runs around the circle and back to his/her seat. Let each child have a turn being the leprechaun. Use the pattern on page 64 to make leprechaun hat nametags or a coloring sheet.
[5 min.]

Internet Site: Heather's Happy St. Patrick's.Day

www.heathersholidaze.com/march/colorpage.html

Print out this leprechaun picture for the children to color. If you hit the link back to "Heather's Happy St. Patrick's Day" page, you will find the history of the holiday, activities, and more. Site by Shade's Landing, Inc.
[5 min.]

Book: *Jamie O'Rourke and the Big Potato*

Retelling of the Irish folktale about the laziest man in Ireland who meets up with a tricky leprechaun. By Tomie DePaola. Putnam, 1992.
[10 min.]

Lucky Leprechauns

Five lucky leprechauns dancing in a ring,
Five lucky leprechauns, hear them sing:
"OOOOO–oooooo–OOOOO!"

Five lucky leprechauns wave their arms high,
Five lucky leprechauns give a loud cry:
"OOOOO–oooooo–OOOOO!"

Five lucky leprechauns in a hollow tree,
Five lucky leprechauns, quiet as can be:
"Shhhhhh–shhhhhh–shhhhhh!"
[Fingerplay—1 min.]

CD-ROM: *Dr. T's Sing-A-Long Around the World*

Sing along with the traditional songs from Ireland. UNI Distribution. [songs]
[5 min.]

How Many Leprechauns?

How many leprechauns do you see?
(shrug shoulder)
Can you count them, 1, 2, 3?
(count on fingers)

How many skinny ones, how many fat?
(use hands to show thin and fat)
How many leprechauns wearing a hat?
(put hands on head)
[Action Rhyme—1 min.]

I'm a Little Leprechaun

(Tune of "I'm a Little Teapot")

I'm a little leprechaun, dressed in green.
I am the tiniest man you have ever seen.
If you can catch me, it is told,
I will give you a pot of gold.
[Song—30 sec.]

Additional Resources to Share

Books

Freeman, Dorothy R. *St. Patrick's Day* (Best Holiday Books). Enslow, 1992. Describes the celebration of Saint Patrick's Day which honors the patron saint of Ireland.

Ross, Kathy. *Crafts for St. Patrick's Day* (Holiday Crafts for Kids). Milbrook Press, 1999. A variety of craft projects suitable for ages 4–8.

Tucker, Kathy. *The Leprechaun in the Basement*. Albert Whitman, 1999. The McKeevers, who are down on their luck, are helped by a leprechaun they find living beneath their home.

Video

The Elves and the Shoemaker. Weston Woods. 6 min. Traditional children's tale of a poor shoemaker who is assisted by the nighttime work of friendly elves.

CD-ROM

Magic Tales Interactive Storybook. Knowledge Adventure/Davidson. Listen to "Liam Finds a Story: An Irish Folktale." [story]

My Card Shop. Wizardwoks. Choose the card for Saint Patrick's Day to paint, stamp, and color. [activities]

Internet Sites

Happy Saint Patricks Rainbow Coloring Page
www.janbrett.com/saint_patricks_coloring_rainbow.htm
This page features a hedgehog and a St. Patrick's Day rainbow to print and color. Illustration by Jan Brett.

VirtualKiss.com: E-Shamrocks
www.thekiss.com/shamrock/
Send an e-mail shamrock to your friends.

pattern for leprechaun hat nametags

Native Americans

Setting the Scene: Exploring Different Cultures

The Internet provides access to historical cultures that kids might not otherwise get to experience. On some sites lines between cultures are blurred, but if approached correctly differences and commonalities can be discovered. Show photos of American Indian dress and talk about the similarities and differences to the children's clothes today.
[4 min.]

Book: *Dreamcatcher*

Based on an Ojibway tradition, this book tells of the weaving of a willow branch and nettle stalk twine dreamcatcher to hang on a baby's cradleboard. By Audrey Osofsky. Orchard, 1992.
[6 min.]

Going on a Buffalo Hunt

We're going on a buffalo hunt,
I'm not afraid.
We're going to get a big one.
We're braves!
Look! What is that ahead?
It's a cave.
Does a buffalo live there?
No!

(Repeat with forest, hills, meadow, etc., until you get to the plains, then see the buffalo, realize how big it is and run away! This is similar to "I'm Going on a Bear Hunt.")
[Song—3 min.]

CD-ROM: *Native American Peoples of the Plains*

Select "Museum" and look at the pages. Read aloud the short captions, such as the information on the tepee. Rainbow Educational Media. [factual information]
[4 min.]

Hiyahiyahoo

See the boy, paddling his canoe—hiyahiyahoo.
See the girl, grinding her corn—hiyahiyaho.
Hiyahiyahooooooooooooooo
[Song—1 min.]

Long Wing Feathers

Wearing my long wingfeathers as I fly,
Wearing my long wingfeathers as I fly,
I circle around,
I circle around,
The boundaries of the earth,
The boundaries of the sky.
(*Repeat the chant and pretend to fly.*)
[Arapaho Chant—1 min.]

Cooking Activity: Oneida Corn Soup

- 1 cup torn, fresh spinach
- 1-15 oz. can of whole kernel corn
- ½ cup chopped cooked beef
- ½ cup log grain rice
- 1 quart water
- 1 tsp. salt
- pepper to taste

Combine ingredients in a medium pot. Simmer until rice is cooked, about 25–30 minutes. Makes 25 small servings. Serve in Styrofoam cups with spoons and napkins.
[10 min.]

✪ Additional Activity: Mosaic

Read *Arrow to the Sun* by Gerald McDermott. Make a giant outline of the boy from the story. Let the children tear various colored pieces of construction paper and glue them on to create a mosaic.

Additional Resources to Share

Books

Grossman, Virginia. *Ten Little Rabbits*. Chronicle, 1991. A counting book featuring rabbits in Native American dress and an added section with facts about Native tribes and clothing.

McDermott, Gerald. *Arrow to the Sun*. Demco Media, 1977. The Caldecott Award-winning tale about Native reverence for the origins of fire.

Medearis, Angela. *Dancing with the Indians*. Holiday House, 1991. An African American girl and her family in the 1930s describe watching a Seminole pow-wow and remember how the tribe befriended her grandfather.

Video

Love Flute. Weston Woods. 9 min. From the book by Paul Goble. In this Plains Indian tale, a shy young man is unable to speak to the girl he loves so he uses a flute to help convey his feelings.

CD-ROM

Magic Tales Interactive Storybook II. Knowledge Adventure/Davidson. Have the children view "Sleeping Cub's Test of Courage: A Native American Folktale." A great moral story for young children. [stories]

The Native Americans. Philips Media. Search the index for Indian clothing and costumes and watch the slide show. [factual information]

Internet Sites

Athabascan Birch Bark Basket
www.teelfamily.com/activities/basket/
This website provides instructions on how to make your own birch bark basket like the Athabascan Indians. Site by the Teel family.

Native American Arts and Crafts
http://iml.jou.ufl.edu/projects/STUDENTS/GREENB/titlpage.html
This site provides history, information and pictures of various Native American arts and crafts. Site by Sarah Greenberg.

Traditional Native American "Hidden Ball" Game
www.bluemountain.com/eng/nativeamer/NAhideb3.html
Click on a stick to guess where the ball is hidden in this online replica of a Zuni game. Can also be sent as an e-card.

No Ghosts

Are You Little Ghosts?

Stand and smile at one another,
Now make a face that would scare your mother!
Jump three times, hop, hop, hop.
Now make a face that would stop a clock.
Show a ghostly face and *Roar!*
And sit yourselves back on the floor.
[Rhyme—2 min.]

CD-ROM: *Awesome Animated Monster Maker*

Go to the lab and select various body parts to create your own custom monsters. Houghton Mifflin Interactive. [activities]
[5 min.]

Five Little Monsters

Five little monsters on a spooky night,
Made a very spooky, scary sight.
The first one danced on his tippy toes,
The next one fell and bumped his nose.
The next one jumped up high in the air,
The next one looked and saw no one was there
And he ran home, but the last one did not care…
Because he's a monster!
[Fingerplay—1 min.]

Book: *One Cow, Moo, Moo!*

A cow and various other farm animals are on the run, but why? By David Bennett. Holt, 1990.
[5 min.]

There Is No Such Thing

(Tune of "Ten Little Indians")

There are no such things as monsters,
Vampires, ghosties, ghouls and goblins.
How do I know this is truthful?
'Cuz my mommy told me so.
[Song—1 min.]

Video: *A Dark, Dark Tale*

Weston Woods. From the book by Ruth Brown. The journey of a black cat across a moor, into the woods, and finally into a gothic mansion where a surprise awaits.
[4 min.]

Internet Site: The Haunted Alphabet

http://www.funschool.com/cgi-bin/ga?kindergarten,i

Click on the "Game Spot" and choose "Haunted Alphabet." Have the kids find the hidden ghostly letters in this game. Site by Funschool Corporation.
[10 min.]

Additional Resources to Share

Books

Nightingale, Sandy. *I'm a Little Monster*. Harcourt Brace, 1995. Tommy's mother says he is a little monster for his messy room, but then the monsters he drew on his wall come to life and show him being one might not be all bad.

Paraskevas, Betty. *Monster Beach*. Harcourt Brace, 1995. Jaunty verse and funny illustrations tell of a boy and his grandfather enjoying the beach until a silly sea monster appears.

Root, Phyllis. *The Hungry Monster*. Candlewick, 1997. A cute monster with scales, wings, and a smile, is looking for a snack.

CD-ROM

GT Interactive. *The Smelly Mystery*. Help Little Monster solve the mystery of the mixed-up smells in Monsterville. [interactive story, games]

Humongous Entertainment. *Pajama Sam: No Need to Hide When It's Dark Outside*. Help Sam confront his fear of the dark with the help of friends he meets along the way. [interactive game]

Internet Sites

GooboWorks: Build a Monster
www.rahul.net/renoir/monster/monster.html
Kids can make their own monsters by clicking on different body parts.

Twentieth Century Fox: Casper's Ghost Cards
www.caspervideo.com/inv/html/invm.html
Have the children send a spooky message to a friend or family member via e-mail with these ghostly postcards.

Nuts!

Game: Squirrel and Nut

During Peanut Butter Lover's Month in November, try this nutty storytime idea. Children sit in a circle, closing their eyes and extending one hand. One child is the "nut" and is given an acorn or walnut to hold. The child who has the nut tiptoes around the circle and puts the nut into an outstretched hand. The "squirrel" who receives the nut opens their eyes, jumps up and chases until the "nut" is caught. Children can take turns being the squirrel and nut.
[5 min.]

Book: *Nuts to You*

An urban squirrel is up to all sorts of tricks as he zips, digs, eats and hides. Lois Ehlert. Harcourt Brace, 1993.
[4 min.])

Chipmunk in a Tree

See the little chipmunk
(hold up left hand, elbow bent)
Run up the tree.
(make right hand "run" up left arm)
There he finds a hole,
(make a hole with hands)
And hides from me.
(cover up eyes to hide)
Watch and you can see him peeking around,
(peek through fingers)
And if you are quiet, *Shhhhh!*
He might come down.
(creep right hand down left)
[Action Rhyme—1 min.]

Internet Site: Nobby Nuss Game

www.scarysquirrel.org/games/nobby

Nobby Nuss the squirrel is getting ready for winter. Help him gather nuts in this online game. Demonstrate, then let the kids try.
[4 min.]

Tony Chestnut

(Tune of "Where Is Thumbkin")

Toe knee chest nut *(head)*
Toe knee chest nut *(head)*
Toe knee nose,
Toe knee nose,
Eye love *(heart)* you *(point)*.
Eye love *(heart)* you *(point)*.
Toe knee nose,
Toe knee nose,
Tony chest nut *(head)*.
(start slow and repeat faster and faster)
[Song—1 min.]

CD-ROM: *Peanut Butter*

This CD-ROM, based on the book *Peanut Butter* by Arlene Erlbach, shows how peanuts are grown, harvested, graded, shelled, and made into peanut butter. Lerner Media. [factual information]
[5 min.]

Five Little Squirrels

Five little squirrels sitting in a tree.
The first one said, "It's getting cold for me."
The second one said, "Leaves are falling to the ground."
The third one said, "Get busy, there's nuts to be found."
The fourth one said, "We better not wait."
The fifth one said, "Fall is really great!"
[Fingerplay—1 min.]

Cooking: Homemade Peanut Butter

Making homemade peanut butter is one way to observe changes and to see a relationship between processed food and raw ingredients. You will need to use an electric blender for quick results. You'll also need the following ingredients:

• 3 cups roasted peanuts in the shell
• 2 teaspoons cooking oil or margarine for smoothness
• salt
• rubber spatula
• plastic bags (optional)

Have the children remove the peanut shells and skins and observe the peanuts. Put the ingredients in the blender and blend till desired consistency. You may need to stop the blender several times to scrape the sides with a spatula.

Place the peanut butter in a plastic bag and cut a hole in one corner to make a squeeze-type bag. The peanut butter can be squeezed into the mouth (astronaut-style) or served on crackers, celery, sliced bananas, apples or small pieces of bread cut with a cookie cutter.

[10 min.]

Activity: Find the Nuts

Make matching sets of squirrels and nuts out of different colored paper. Laminate the shapes. Hide the nuts throughout the room. Give each child a squirrel and send them out on a hunt to find the nut of the same color.

[5 min. or more]

✪ Additional Activity: Nutty Books

Using the pattern below, enlarge and cut peanut-shaped pages from brown construction paper. Punch holes in the pages and tie with yarn. The kids glue a peanut on each page and draw the face according to the following rhyme. Kids love them!

Nuts

(Rhyme to use with nutty books)

Sad nuts
Mad nuts
Glad nuts
I like nuts!

Additional Resources to Share

Books

Browne, Eileen. *Tick Tock*. Candlewick, 1994. Two squirrels try to make a clock work.

Cooper, Patrick. *Never Trust a Squirrel*. Dutton, 1999. William the guinea pig tries life outside the cage with the help of a friendly but unreliable squirrel.

Erlbach, Arlen. *Peanut Butter*. Lerner, 1997. How peanut butter is made from growing the nuts to the factory process.

Pallotta, Jerry. *Reeses Pieces Peanut Butter: Counting Board Book*. Corporate Board Books, 1999.

CD-ROM

Peanuts Picture Puzzler. Multicom. Complete the puzzles to see the pictures become animated. [games]

Shelly Duvall's It's a Bird's Life. Sanctuary Woods. Go to the games and play the "Peanut Under the Shell" game.

Internet Sites

Planter's Company: Relax and Go Nuts
www.planters.com
This site contains the history of Planters, nutritional information about peanuts, recipes, and more.

Walnuts Game
members.aol.com/steadle/walnuts.htm
Download this free shareware game for any version of Windows. Move the basket back and forth and try to catch all the walnuts dropped by the squirrel

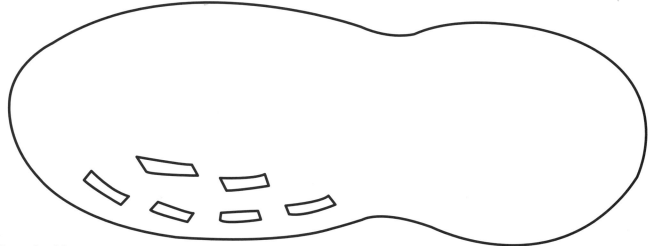

"nutty book" pattern

Penguins

Setting the Scene: Let's Talk About Penguins

Penguins don't fly. They waddle upright on short legs, and they are great swimmers. The smallest penguin is the Little Blue, which is sixteen inches tall and weighs two pounds. The largest penguin is the Emperor, which stands 45 inches tall and weighs up to 90 pounds. Help kids visualize penguin size by using a yardstick marked with the height of the Little Blue and Emperor species.
[4 min.]

Internet Site: The Penguin Page

http://home.capu.net/~kwelch/pp/species/emperor.html

Scroll to the bottom of the page and click on the projector icon to watch a penguin migration. Or, click on the speaker icon to hear penguins bickering. The penguin fact sheets have beautiful pictures and lots of information for parents.
[3 min.]

I Know a Little Penguin

I know a little penguin
Who sat on an ice block.
He swam in the ocean
And waddled on the rocks.

He snapped at a sea gull,
He snapped at a seal,
He snapped at a fish—
Oh, what a meal!
[Fingerplay—1 min.]

Book: *The Emperor Penguin's New Clothes*

The traditional tale retold with penguin characters. Janet Perlman. Viking, 1994.
[4 min.]

Penguin, Penguin

Waddle, waddle, waddle,
From side to side.
Penguins go a walking,
Slip, slip, slide!

With a funny jump,
The penguins dash
Down to the water,
Splash, splash, splash!
[Rhyme—1 min.]

CD-ROM: *EarthQuest: Polar Trek*

Explore the wonders of the polar region, its icy landscape, and fascinating creatures. This CD has photos, narration and video. Choose "Image Library" from the icons across the top for photos of penguins and other arctic animals or "Video Library" for video clips of penguins and more. Andromeda Software. [factual information]
[4 min.]

I'm a Little Penguin

(Tune of "I'm a Little Teapot")

I'm a little penguin
Round and sleek.
Here is my tummy
And here is my beak.

The snow is falling,
The ice is thin,
Watch me as I jump right in!
[1 min.]

Craft: Penguin Vest

Use large grocery sacks and orange construction paper to make vests. Slit the front of the bag from top to bottom. Cut a neck hole in the bottom of the bag. With crayons, color the bag black and white to resemble a penguin. Cut a flap on each side to resemble wings. Cut a triangular piece of orange paper and shape a cone from it. Staple it closed and punch one hole on each side of the bottom of the cone. Thread a 12" piece of yarn through each hole. Place the cone over your nose like a beak and tie the yarn behind the head. (See illustration on page 71.)
[10 min.]

✪ Additional Activity: Iceberg Game

Mark circles with masking tape on the floor of your story area. Separate the children into groups of three. Ask the children to pretend to be penguins, and tell them that the circles are the iceberg. Start out with one child in each circle. When you yell "Waddle!" the children must try to find a circle to stand in, with no more than three penguins to an iceberg at a time. Those who are left when you yell "Stop!" must sit down until the next round.

Additional Resources to Share

Books

Alborough, Jez. *Cuddly Duddly*. Candlewick, 1993. Duddly leaves his penguin family because they just like to cuddle too much.

Atwater, Richard. *Mr. Popper's Penguins*. Little, Brown, 1992. A classic of American humor, the adventures of a housepainter and his brood of high-stepping penguins have delighted children for generations.

Lester, Helen. *Tacky in Trouble*. Houghton Mifflin, 1997. Tacky tries his hand at sailboarding and accidentally ends up on a tropical island with a lion.

CD-ROM

Penny Penguin's Math Bingo. Lattice Works Software. Play Bingo using the counting mode on level one. Play Bingo against Penny Penguin. [math game]

Internet Sites

Iceblox
  www.tdb.uu.se/~karl/java/iceblox.html
  Download this game and help Pixel Pete the penguin collect coins among the ice blocks and avoid the flames. Game from Karl Hornell.

Penguin Links
  www.stemnet.nf.ca/~mwhitt/penguin/penguin.html
  This site contains links to other sites containing stories, pictures and information about penguins. Site by Michael Witt.

penguin vest

Pig Tales

Game: Pin the Snout on the Pig

Cut a 15" circle from pink poster board. Draw ears and facial features on the circle to create a face, but do not draw a mouth. Cut 4" circles from construction paper and draw nostrils on them to use as snouts. Invite the children to tape the snouts on in the same way "Pin the Tail on the Donkey" is played. Use the pattern on page 73 to make pig nametags or a coloring sheet.
[5 min.]

Book: *The Pig in the Pond*

The charming tale of how Neligan's pig spends a hot day. By Martin Waddell. Candlewick, 1992.
[4 min.]

Pig in a Pen

Pig in a pen, count to ten.
(hold up ten fingers)
Pig in a tree, count to three.
(hold up three fingers)
Pig out the door, count to four.
(hold up four fingers)
[Action Rhyme—I min.]

CD-ROM: *Stamped on Fairy Tales: Pigs*

Retelling of a classic tale with animation and music. Kids can interactively plot new endings to the story. Enteractive, Inc. {interactive story]
[5 min.]

Internet Site: Three Little Pigs

www.heritagestudio.com/3pigs.htm

D.J. Neary's original illustrations of the *Three Little Pigs*. Site by Fiona Neary of Heritage Studios.
[4 min.]

Pig Rap

This is a story by old Mother Goose
About three little pigs who were on the loose.
The first little pig built a house of straw,
The shakiest house that you ever saw!

Chorus:
The big bad wolf said "Let me come in!"
"Oh, not by the hair of my chinny-chin-chin."
"Then I'll huff and puff and blow your house in!"
So he huffed *(snap twice)*
And he puffed *(snap twice)*
And the little pig ran to the second pig's house.

The second pig built a house out of sticks
But the bad old wolf was still up to his tricks.

Chorus *(change the word second to third in the last line)*

The third little pig built his house of bricks
And that was much stronger than straw or sticks.

Chorus *(change the last line to "But the pigs stayed in the third pig's house.")*

The big bad wolf said "Let me come in,
Or I'll climb down the chimney and do you in."

Chorus *(same as above)*

Pig said "Come in, come in
We'll be ready for you,
And you'll never guess what we will do."
So the pigs made a fire, red hot
and boiled water in a big black pot.
And he slid *(snap twice)*
And he slid *(snap twice)*
Down in the water in the middle of the night—
But that is okay, 'cause it served him right!
[Rap—I min.]

Internet Site: Babirusa

www.stlzoo.org/content.asp?page_name=babirusa

Pictures and background information on this elusive member of the pig family. Site by the St. Louis Zoo.
[5 min.]

Book: *Pigs Aplenty, Pigs Galore*

A rhyming tale about a group of uninvited pig guests. By David McPhail. Dutton, 1993.
[4 min.]

Additional Resources to Share

Books

Meddaugh, Susan. *Five Little Piggies*. Candlewick, 1998. The true, expanded version of the favorite children's rhyme.

Palatini, Margie. *Piggie Pie*. Clarion, 1995. A witch tries to get all the ingredients she needs to make piggy pie.

Thompson, Carol. *Piggy Washes Up*. Candlewick, 1997. Kids will identify with Piggy's bathtime ritual.

CD-ROM

Little Red Hen. Create a story using the pig stamp. Contains pages that can also be printed out and used as coloring sheets. Learning Tree House, Interactive Storytime Vol. I. [interactive story]

The World of Totty Pig: You Are Much Too Small. Byron Preiss Multimedia. Based on the book *You Are Much Too Small* by Betty Boegehold, listen to the story and sing along. [story]

Internet Sites

Enchanted Learning Software: This Little Piggy
www.enchantedlearning.com/rhymes/Piggies.shtml
This site contains the rhyme "This Little Piggy" in rebus form.

pattern for pig nametag and coloring sheet

Pirate Pals

Setting the Scene: Let's Look Like Pirates

For this storytime, wear a red and white striped t-shirt, jeans rolled to the knees, a bandanna tied around your head, a gold hoop earring and a mustache drawn with eyeliner pencil. Make pirate hats using the instructions on page 75. Cut out the skull and glue to the front of the hat.
[7 min.]

CD-ROM: *The Pirate Who Would Not Wash*

Listen to the tale of Pongo the Pirate, who is so smelly even the rats on his ship desert him. Packard Bell. Kidstory Learning Series. [story]
[5 min.]

Pirate, Pirate

Pirate, pirate, as mean as can be,
(make a fierce expression)
Lives on a ship,
(make bow shape with hands)
And sails on the sea.
(make a motion like waves with one hand)

He buries his treasure
Under the sand,
(pretend to dig)
And then sails away as fast as he can.
(make bow shape again)
[Action Rhyme—1 min.]

Book: *Jolly Roger and the Pirates of Captain Abdul*

A funny tale about smelly, hairy, and scary pirates. By Colin McNaughton. Candlewick, 1995.
[5 min.]

The Very Scary Pirate

(Tune of "The Itsy Bitsy Spider")

The very scary pirate climbed aboard a ship,
He took out his sword and gave the crew a trip.
Then he saw the sail and ripped it with his sword,
But I came to the rescue and threw him overboard.
[Song—1 min.]

Book: *Pirate School*

Ahoy, mates! It's all aboard the P.S. 1. At Pirate School, would-be pirates train to be tough! There's no crying and no name-calling, but there's always plenty of fighting. Laughs and adventure abound in this funny story for seafarers and landlubbers alike. By Kathy East Dubowsky. Grosset and Dunlap, 1996.
[6 min.]

Internet Site: Luke Saves the Day

www.powerup.com.au/~glen/pirate4aaa.htm

Read this online story about kids who have a run-in with pirates.
[4 min.]

Additional Resources to Share

Books

Hutchins, Pat. *One-Eyed Jake*. Greenwillow, 1979. A greedy pirate plunders one ship too many.

McCully, Emily Arnold. *The Pirate Queen*. Putnam, 1996. The true story of an female Irish pirate.

McNaughton, Colin. *Captain Abdul's Pirate School*. Candlewick, 1994. Captain Abdul starts his own school for kids who want to become pirates when they grow up.

CD-ROM

Fisher Price Pirate Ship. Davidson and Associates. Practice shooting a cannon and search for missing pieces of the treasure map. [activities]

Safety Scavenger Hunt. Starr Press Multimedia. Go to Rosie Raccoon's house and find the unsafe features in her room. Use the treasure map to find the hidden treasure. [safety information, activities]

Internet Sites

KidsTV: Make a Pirate Hat
www.kidstv.co.nz/makehat.html
Easy, complete instructions on making a pirate hat.

Thinkquest: Pirates!
http://library.thinkquest.org/16438/fact/pirate_ships.shtml
Explore pirate ship words, kinds of vessels, and lots of facts and fiction.

Pirate Hat

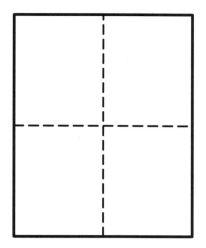

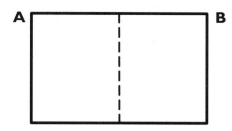

1. Begin with a rectangle (a sheet of newspaper makes a good hat). Fold in half lengthwise and unfold, then fold in half crosswise.

2. Fold corners A and B so they meet at the center crease line.

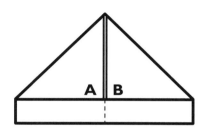

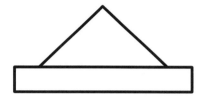

3. Fold bottom flap up so that the crease is along corners A and B. Turn paper over and repeat.

4. Copy skull onto white paper. Cut out and glue on front of hat.

Sign Language

Setting the Scene: Introduction to Sign Language

Very young children can learn signs before they begin to talk, improving their ability to communicate and encouraging other learning. You can read more about this in the book *Baby Signs: How to Talk to Your Baby Before Your Baby Can Talk* by Linda Acredelo and Susan Goodwyn (Contemporary Books, 1996). For a simple introduction to American Sign Language, try Cindy Wheeler's *Simple Signs* (Puffin, 1997). This book has 28 simple word signs—such as cat, dog, eat and happy. Each sign comes with easy-to-understand directions on how to place or move the hands ("like pedaling a bike," "like peeling a banana," etc.) **[7 min.]**

CD-ROM: *Interactive Sign Language: Fingerspelling and Numbers*

Click on the "Learn Signs" button. Then click on the button labeled "ABC" and choose a letter to see it signed. Palantine, Inc. [factual information, activities] **[10 min.]**

Springtime: A Song for the Other Senses

(Tune of "Did You Ever See a Lassie?")

(Discuss how kids might experience seasons changing without hearing, then sing this song.)

My eyes can see it's springtime,
It's springtime, it's springtime.
My eyes can see it's springtime,
The grass is so green.

My nose can smell it's springtime,
It's springtime, it's springtime.
My nose can smell it's springtime,
The flowers smell sweet.

My body knows it's springtime,
It's springtime, it's springtime,
My body knows it's springtime,
The air is so warm.
[Song—I min.]

I Love You

Hold up five fingers, *(hold up fingers)*
Now bend down two. *(bend down middle and ring finger, leave index finger, pinkie and thumb out)*
Do you know what you are saying?
"I Love You."
[Fingerplay—I min.]

Internet Site: Sign Language Page

www.clandjop.com/~brown/sign.html

This site shows the hand sign for "I Love You." Site by Ami Brown.
[3 min.]

Book: *Moses Goes to a Concert*

Moses and his classmates who are deaf attend a concert featuring a percussionist who is also deaf. By Isaac Millman. Farrar, Strauss & Giroux, 1998.
[5 min.]

Additional Resources to Share

Books

Addabbo, Carol. *Dina the Deaf Dinosaur.* Hannacroix Creek Books, 1997. Dina is lost in the woods until she is befriended by Moliere the mole, Camilla the chipmunk, and Otto, an owl who knows sign language.

_____. *Word Signs: A First Book of Sign Language.* Gallaudet University, 1995. Color photos show signs for basic words and animals.

Video

Sing N Sign for Fun. Gaia, 42 min. A variety of songs are sung and signed by kids.

CD-ROM

Paws Signs Stories. Institute for Disablilities Research and Training. A literature-based CD-ROM featuring stories and games using American Sign Language handshapes, fingerspelling, and facial grammar.

Sign Language for Everyone. IVI Publishing. Watch animations of select phrases signed.

Internet Sites

ASL Spelling Study: The Alphabet
www.sirius.com/~dub/CALL/asl.html
Play a guessing game with the signed letters. Site by Jim Duber.

Animated Sign Language Dictionary.
www.bconnex.net/~randys/index_nf.html
This animated dictionary shows kids how to sign specific words. It also contains links to other sites related to ASL and deaf culture. Site by Randy Stine.

Squiggly Wiggly Tales

Setting the Scene: Sing a Song of Worms

As the children enter the storytime area, teach them the song "Squiggly, Wiggly Worm" with appropriate hand motions.

Squiggly, Wiggly Worm

(Tune of "The Itsy Bitsy Spider")

The squiggly wiggly worm *(wiggle fingers)*
Went crawling underground. *(crawl fingers up arm)*
Down came the rain, *(flicker fingers down)*
And mud was all around. *(make smoothing motion)*
Rain filled the tunnels *(make circle with arms)*
And pushed out the wiggly worm. *(wiggle fingers)*
So the puddles on the ground *(wiggle fingers)*
Were the only place to squirm. *(wiggle fingers)*
[Song—1 min.]

Book: *Inch by Inch*

An inchworm is proud of his ability to measure things, and saves himself from a hungry bird with that very skill. By Leo Lionni. Mulberry, 1995.
[5 min.]

Wiggly Worm

Wiggly, wiggly, wiggly worm,
(wiggle whole body as words direct)
Wiggles out of the earth so firm.
He wiggles fast,
He wiggles slow.
Then back into
The earth he goes.
[Action Rhyme—30 sec.]

Book: *A Worm's Tale*

Arthur gains a new friend after accidentally stepping on a worm in the park. By Barbro Lindgren. R & S, 1988.
[5 min.]

Internet Site: WormWorld

www.nj.com/yucky/worm

Get all the "dirt" on worms at this site. Part of the Yuckiest Site on the Internet from New Jersey Online.
[7 min.]

Wiggle Worm

Do you always have to wiggle? *(wiggle in chair)*
Do you always have to squirm?
You wiggle and jiggle, *(wiggle and jiggle)*
Like a regular worm. *(wiggle hand)*

You wiggle in your chair, *(wiggle in chair)*
And you wiggle in your bed.
You wiggle with your legs, *(wiggle legs)*
And you wiggle with your head. *(wiggle head)*

You wiggle with your hands, *(wiggle hands)*
And you wiggle with your feet. *(wiggle feet)*
You wiggle when you're playing,
And you wiggle when you eat.

I guess you're made to wiggle, *(everyone wiggle)*
And I guess you're made to squirm.
So I'll like the wiggle, jiggle,
And I'll love my wiggle worm.
[Action Rhyme—1 min.]

Action Game: Snail

Have the children form a line and hold hands. As the verses below are recited, lead the line into a spiral, which gets smaller and tighter and then unwinds to form a line again.

Snail Rhyme

Hand in hand, you see us well,
Slow like a snail into his shell.
Ever nearer, ever closer,
Very snugly do you dwell
Snail within your tiny shell.

Hand in hand, you see us well,
Slow like a snail out of his shell.
Ever farther, ever wider,
Who'd have thought this tiny shell
Could have held a snail so well?
[5 min.]

Craft: Worm Bookmarks

Using the pattern on page 80, outline the worm in marker on a piece of felt and cut out. Have the children use markers to add facial features and other details.
[6+ min.]

Additional Resources to Share

Books

Edwards, Pamela. *Some Smug Slug*. HarperCollins, 1996. A slug gets into trouble by not paying attention to his surroundings.

Greenberg, David. *Slugs*. Little, Brown, 1983. A humorous rhyme about the uses of slugs.

CD-ROM

Math Blaster. Knowledge Adventure. Shrink and stretch then count the glow worms. For first grade. [learning games]

Multimedia Bug Book. Workman Swift. Help Dr. Anson Pantz find and identify bugs. [factual information, activities]

Space Worms. Little Fingers Software. Choose "Earth Worms" and guess which of the worms shown need a ride back to earth. [game]

Internet Sites

Snail's Race Game
www.europa.com/~doomer/shuskey/example1.html
Race the different colored snails in this game. Click on the color dice in the left corner and the corresponding snail will move toward the finish line. Game by Scott Huskey.

Urban Programs Resource Network: The Adventures of Herman
www.urbanext.uiuc.edu/worms/
Meet Squirmin' Herman the worm and learn all about his life, surroundings and habits. Also contains worm facts, worm links, games, activities and more.

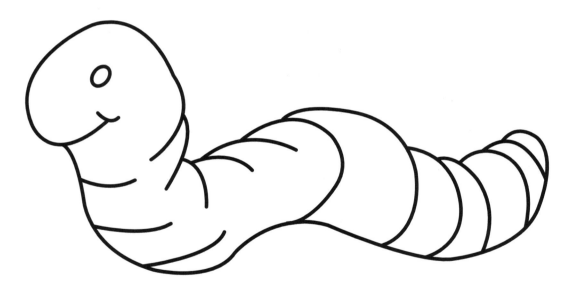

pattern for worm bookmark

Starry Nights

Setting the Scene: Star Sites and Sounds

The universe is one billion years old, but there is always something new in space. There are some excellent Internet sites created by NASA and other organizations that show kids what is "up there." (Check out the "Space Place" in the Internet Resources on p. 78.) Play the theme from *Star Wars* while the kids enter the story area. Use the star pattern on this page to make nametags.
[3 min.]

Internet Site: Space ABCs

buckman.pps.k12.or.us/room100/abcspace/spacebox.html

An online alphabet book with sound. From students at Buckman Elementary School, Portland, Oregon.
[4 min.]

A Trip to Mars

Let's look at the moon.
(circle arms over head)
Let's look at the stars.
(wiggle fingers over head)
Let's get in our rocket ship.
(crouch down with hands in prayer position over head)
Let's blast off to Mars!
(jump up and push arms up high)
[Action Rhyme—1 min.]

Book: *I Want to Be an Astronaut*

A young child imagines what it would be like to go on a mission to space. By Byron Barton. Crowell, 1988.
[4 min.]

Ring around a Rocket

Ring around a rocket,
(join hands and walk in a circle)
Try to catch a star.
(make grasping motions towards the sky)
The stars are falling
(fall to the floor)
Right where you are.
[Action Rhyme—1 min.]

Book: *Twinkle, Twinkle, Little Star*

An expanded version of the popular children's poem. By Isa Trapini. Whispering Coyote, 1994.
[6 min.]

Science Activity: Balloon Rocket

Demonstrate how a rocket works. Decorate a paper lunch sack with copies of the rocket pattern on page 78. Blow up an 8" balloon and hold closed. Place the sack over the rounded end of the balloon. Have a "count down" and let the balloon go.
[4 min.]

Craft: Glitter Stars

For this craft, you will need a 6" wax paper square for each child, white craft glue, paper towels and glitter.

Place each wax paper square on a paper towel. Have the children squeeze lines of glue on the wax paper to form the outlines of stars. Sprinkle glitter on the glue lines. Let the glue dry thoroughly. When the stars are dry, they will peel off the wax paper. They can be hung in the window as decorations.
[7 min.]

Book: *I Like Stars*

"Red stars. Yellow stars. I like stars." This wonderful, easy-to-read poem is filled with rich, vibrant imagery. By Joan Paley. Golden Books, 1998.
[3 min.]

pattern for star nametag

Additional Resources to Share

Books

Cole, Norma. *Blast Off! A Space Counting Book.* Charlesbridge, 1994. Numbers are represented by objects and words related to space.

Sharrat, Nick. *Rocket Countdown.* Candlewick, 1995. This flap and pop-up book features a countdown before a rocket launch.

Vagin, Vladimir. *Insects from Outer Space.* Scholastic, 1995. An invasion of insects from another planet disrupts the Earth Bug Dance.

Cassettes

I Want to Be an Astronaut. Twin Sisters, 1997. Original songs about space, stars, and being an astronaut.

Williams, John. *Star Wars: A New Hope, The Original Motion Picture Soundtrack.* RCA Victor, 1997.

Video

The Magic School Bus Gets Lost in Space. PBS, 30 min.

CD-ROM

Alistair and the Alien Invasion Storybook. Living Books. Alistair searches the universe for a plant for a school assignment. Listen to the tale of his adventures on the Twickadily planet. [interactive story]

Allie's Playhouse. Opcode Interactive. Start the program and view the main playhouse screen. Select the planet icon and match the planet names with the pictures. [activities, games]

Putt Putt Goes to the Moon. Humongous Entertainment. This game has kids drive Putt Putt the car to the moon, where he meets the mayor and explores the moon. [interactive game]

Internet Sites

California Institute of Technology: Space Place
http://spaceplace.jpl.nasa.gov/spacepl.htm
Explore this entire site for space facts, fun, activities and more.

Students for the Exploration and Development of Space
http://seds.lpl.arizona.edu/nineplanets/nineplanets/nineplanets.html
Take a tour of the nine planets. Contains loads of information, images, sounds, movies and more.

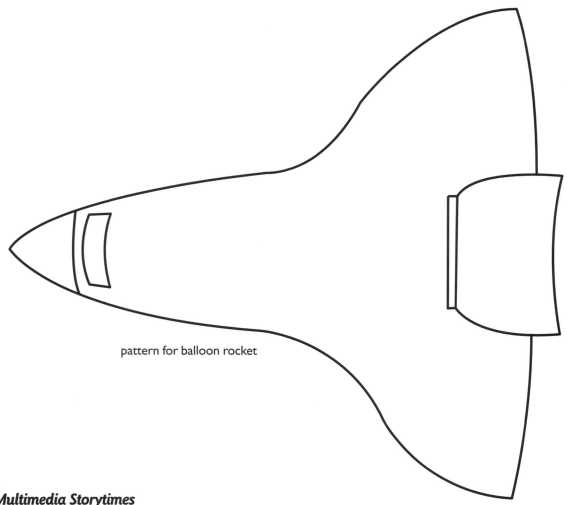

pattern for balloon rocket

Tooth Fairy

Setting the Scene: Tooth Talk

Ask the children what their teeth are for and what it would be like to not have any teeth. Tell them to count their teeth and see if everyone has the same number. Ask if anyone has lost any teeth and if they know who the Tooth Fairy is.
[4 min.]

Book: *Little Rabbit's Loose Tooth*

After Little Rabbit's tooth finally falls out, she does not believe that the tooth fairy will really come. By Lucy Bates. Crown, 1975.
[6 min.]

I Have a Loose Tooth

I have a loose tooth,
A wiggly jiggly loose tooth,
Hanging by a thread.

So I pulled my loose tooth,
My wiggly, jiggly loose tooth,
And then I went to bed.

The fairy took my loose tooth,
My wiggly, jiggly loose tooth,
And now I have a quarter instead.
[Rhyme—45 sec.]

CD-ROM: *My Amazing Human Body*

Help Seemore Skinless the skeleton explore the mouth and teeth. Dorling Kindersley Multimedia. [factual information, activities]
[6 min.]

Book: *The Tooth Witch*

A small, sweet witch does not like stealing the lost teeth of children, so she leaves them gifts under their pillows. By Nurit Karlin. Harper Trophy, 1995.
[4 min.]

Brush Your Teeth

(Tune of "Row, Row, Row Your Boat")

Brush, brush, brush your teeth,
Brush the germs away.

Happy, healthy teeth you will have
By brushing every day.
[1 min.]

Game: Pin the Tooth in the Mouth

Using the patterns on page 82, enlarge and cut a smile shape from white poster board. Draw on red lips and outline teeth with black. Choose one tooth to color black to represent a "missing" tooth. Cut teeth from white paper and give one to each child with a small circle of tape. Play as you would "Pin the Tail on the Donkey."
[Song—10 min.]

Got My Toothpaste

Got my toothpaste, got my brush,
(hold up one finger, then two)
I won't hurry, I won't rush.
(shake head)
Making sure my teeth are clean,
(smile)
Front and back and in between.
(point to teeth)
When I brush for quite a while
(pretend to brush)
I have such a happy smile.
(show teeth in a smile)
[Action Rhyme—1 min.]

Internet Site: Dr. Rabbit's No Cavity Clubhouse

www.colgate.com/kids-world/index.html

This site is loaded with tooth facts, fun games, brushing charts and more. You can even have the kids e-mail the tooth fairy and receive a reply. Site by Colgate Palmolive Company.
[3 min.]

✪ Additional Activity: Paper Plate Mouth

Cut 8" paper plates in half. Make hinges with clear tape on the outside of the plate and tape the halves together. Color the inside of the plates pink. Cut tongues from red construction paper and teeth from white paper and tape these to the inside. Glue button eyes and a cotton ball nose to the top of the plate.

Additional Resources to Share

Book

Luppens, Michel. *What Do Fairies Do with All Those Teeth?* Firefly, 1996. An imaginative look at the uses for lost teeth.

Cassette

Raffi. *Singable Songs for the Very Young* . Uni/Rounder. Features the song "Brush Your Teeth."

Video

Tooth Fairy. Audrey Wood's Child's Play Theater, 10 min. From the book by Audrey Wood. When Matthew loses a tooth, Jessica decides to take advantage of the Tooth Fairy's visit.

CD-ROM

What Is a Bellybutton? Dorling Kindersley Multimedia. Click on the doorknob and play the game "Which Creatures Have Teeth?" [factual information, learning games]

Where Did My Toothbrush Go? D.C. Heath. Kids play this flannelboard-like game by moving objects and adding text to a toothbrush story. [factual information, learning activities]

Internet Sites

Tooth Fairy Page
www.toothfairy.org
Here you can finds tons of dental links, Tooth Fairy FAQs and oral hygiene tips. Site by Megan McCormack, a dental hygienist.

Tooth Fairy Tales: Bad Breath Invasion
www.iuma.com/IUMA/Bands/Tooth_Fairy_Tales/
Listen to this online tale about Molar the dog who wanders away from the city of Teeth. Must have RealPlayer or mp3 to listen to this story.

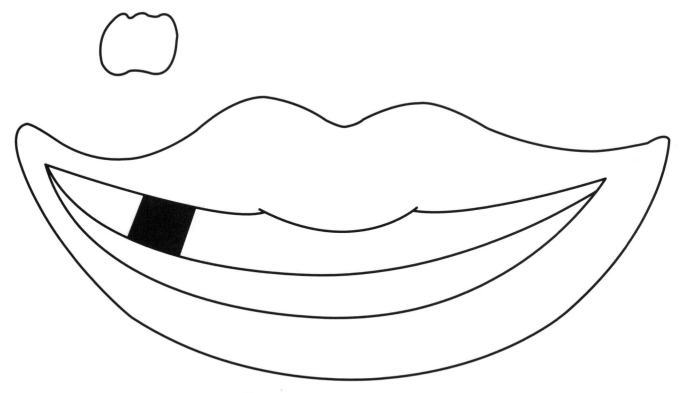

"Pin the Tooth in the Mouth" patterns

Trains

Setting the Scene: Train Tales

Introduce the topic of trains by reading *Freight Train* by Donald Crews. This book provides some basic information on the names of the train cars.
[5 min.]

Here Is the Engine

(Lift each finger as recited.)
Here is the engine on the track.
Here is the coal car just in back.
Here is the boxcar to carry the freight.
Here is the mail car, don't be late.
Way back here through the sun and the rain
Rides the caboose at the end of the train.
[Fingerplay—45 sec.]

Book: *The Train Ride*

A rhyming story that creates a rhythm that simulates the gentle motion of a train. By Stephen Lambert. Candlewick, 1995.
[4 min.]

Little Red Caboose

Little red caboose, chug, chug, chug.
(rub palms together)
Little red caboose, chug, chug, chug.
Little red caboose behind the train, train, train.
(point over shoulder with thumb)
With a smokestack on his back, back, back.
(pat yourself on the back)
Coming around the track, track, track.
Little red caboose behind the train—*Whoooo!*
(pretend to pull whistle)
[1 min.]

Internet Site: Fun with Trains

www.meddybemps.com/9.411.html

A simple activity about counting, size and opposites. Children look at the trains in the parade and answer simple questions. From the Chateau Meddybemps website by Jerry Jindrich.
[4 min.]

CD-ROM: *Kidstory Series: The Little Engine That Could*

The well-known story about a little engine who achieves big things. Packard Bell. [story]
[5 min.]

Craft: Train Stick Puppets

Copy the train pattern on page 84 onto stiff paper and cut out. Have children color the train and tape it to a craft stick to make a puppet.
[5 min.]

Internet Site: Thomas and Friends

www.thomasthetankengine.com

Show the kids the *Thomas the Tank Engine* site as they leave the storytime. Have some Thomas books on hand for check out. Site by Britt Alcroft Company.
[1 min.]

Additional Resources to Share

Books

Carle, Eric. *1, 2, 3, to the Zoo*. Philomel, 1982. Each car on the train has one more zoo animal than the one before it, from one elephant to ten birds.

Crews, Donald. *Freight Train*. Greenwillow, 1978. A pictorial work about a train engine and its cars.

Gibbons, Gail. *Trains*. Henry Holt, 1987. This book describes trains and their uses.

Lewis, Kim. *The Last Train*. Candlewick, 1994. A lyrical tale about Sara and James, who imagine the last railroad train to go by an abandoned hut.

CD-ROM

Nikolai's Train. Corel CD Home. Race on a train with Nikolai and his cat, Neow-Neow. [stories, games]

Polar Express by Chris VanAllsburg. Houghton Mifflin. Listen to the narration and watch the animation based on the wonderful Christmas book about a boy who rides a magical train to meet Santa Claus. [story]

Internet Sites

University of Ulm: Interactive Model Railroad
http://rr-vs.informatik.uni-ulm.de/rr/
On this site you can run a model railroad from your computer.

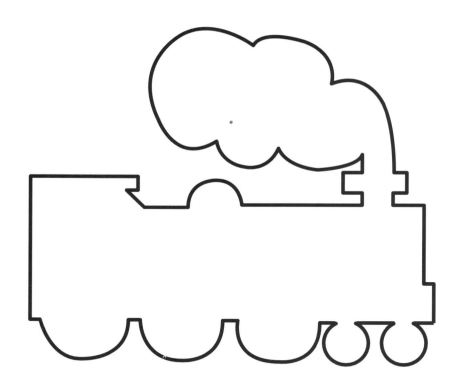

pattern for train puppet

Turtle Tales

Setting the Scene: Sing a Turtle Tune

As the children enter the story area, teach them "The Turtle Pond" song with appropriate motions. Sung to "Here We Go Round the Mulberry Bush."

The Turtle Pond

(Tune of "Here We Go Round the Mulberry Bush")

Let's go to the turtle pond (*"swim" hand*)
The turtle pond, the turtle pond,
Let's go to the turtle pond
So early in the morning. (*raise arms over head*)

Additional verses:
This is the way the turtle crawls…
(*"crawl" hand*)
This is the way he carries his shell…
(*put one hand on the back of the other*)
This is the way he snaps a fly…
(*make pinching motion with hand*)
[Song—3 min.]

Book: *In the Middle of the Puddle*

A frog and turtle watch as their puddle is transformed by a sudden rain. By Mike Thaler. Harper and Row, 1988.
[4 min.]

Turtle

(Cup hands to form turtle and move as described.)
Turtle sticks his neck out so he can see.
He looks and says "Come along with me."
We go very slowly then stop and rest.
Turtles don't go quickly, but they do their best.
We go forward again, very slowly—
That is the way that turtles go.
[Fingerplay—1 min.]

CD-ROM: *Sammy's Science House*

Choose spring at Acorn Pond and watch the turtle lay an egg. Follow the egg's progression through the other seasons. Edmark.
[4 min.]

Book: *The Foolish Tortoise*

A tortoise realizes his need for a shell after several scary encounters. Richard Buckley, Illustrated by Eric Carle. Little Simon, 1998.
[5 min.]

The Turtle

The turtle wears a shell on her back,
(*pat back*)
She walks very slow.
(*creep hand on arm slowly*)
But put her in the water and watch
Just how fast she can go!
(*"swim" hand quickly*)
[Action Rhyme—1 min.]

Book: *Tricky Tortoise*

Tortoise outsmarts elephant by proving he can jump over elephant's "tiny, stupid head." By Mwenye Hadithi, et al. Little, Brown, 1988.
[6 min.]

Internet Site: Turtle Coloring Sheet

www.SquiglysPlayhouse.com/ArtsAndCrafts/
ColouringPictures/Turtle.html
This site contains a picture of a turtle for kids to print and color. From the Squigly's Playhouse site by Barb Willner. Or, you can use the pattern on page 86 for a coloring sheet or nametags.
[4 min.]

Additional Resources to Share

Books

Asch, Frank. *Turtle Tale*. 1978. A turtle has a series of mishaps after sticking his head out of his shell.

George, William T. *Box Turtle at Long Pond*. Greenwillow, 1989. A recounting of a day in the life of a box turtle. Illustrated with very detailed and beautiful nature paintings.

Jay, Lorraine A. *Sea Turtle Journey: The Story of a Loggerhead Turtle*. Soundprints, 1995. This story tells about the life cycle of Hatchling, a baby loggerhead.

Video

Sea Turtle Adventures. Audubon's Animal Adventures. 30 min. Documentary about the birth and life of sea turtles.

CD-ROM

Blue Tortoise. Corel CD Home. Watch and listen to this story of a tortoise on a picnic. [story]

Franklin's Reading World. Sanctuary Woods. Select objects and practice spelling on the pages featuring Franklin the turtle. [stories and games]

Internet Sites

Kidz Corner: Sea Turtles for Kids
www.turtles.org/kids.htm
Stories, poems, essays and activities about turtles.

Nickelodian Jr.: Franklin Online
www.nickjr.com/franklin/
Meet Franklin the Turtle and his friends. This site is filled with activities, pictures, movies and more. Need MediaPlayer for the movies.

pattern for turtle nametag or coloring sheet

Wiggle and Hop (All About Rabbits)

Activity: Animal Cracker Sort

Animal crackers can be used to sort and match. Dump a large pile of crackers on a table. Have the children sort the different animals separate piles. Remember to look for rabbits! When you finish, eat the crackers, of course. Use the patterns on page 88 to make rabbit nametags or a coloring sheet.
[5 min.]

Internet Site: The Tortoise and the Hare

www.ipl.org/youth/StoryHour/

Choose "The Tortoise and the Hare" from the list of stories and let one or two kids page through this well-known tale. Site from the Internet Library.
[4 min.]

Hop Like a Bunny

(hop as described)
Hop like a bunny, hop, hop, hop!
Hop like a bunny, please don't stop.
Hop on your left foot,
Now on your right.
Hop very high with all of your might.
Hop like a bunny, hop, hop, hop.
Are you tired? It's time to stop.
[Action Rhyme—1 min.]

Book: *Do Bunnies Talk?*

This humorous rhyme describes what sounds rabbits do not make. By Dayle Dodds. HarperCollins, 1992.
[6 min.]

I'm a Little Bunny

(Tune of "I'm a Little Teapot")

I'm a little bunny with a fluffy tail,
See me hopping down the trail.
When I pass a carrot, my ears will shake
And then, of course, a bite I'll take.
[1 min.]

Book: *Let's Make Rabbits*

The classic tale of rabbits made with scissors and wall paper scraps. By Leo Lionni. Pantheon, 1982.
[4 min.]

Bunny

Here comes a bunny, hop, hop, hop.
(hop)
See his ears go flop, flop, flop.
(put hands close to ears and flop back and forth)
See his nose go twink, twink, twink.
(wiggle nose with finger)
See his eyes go wink, wink, wink.
(wink)
[Action Rhyme—2 min.]

Craft: Let's Make Rabbits

Use the book *Let's Make Rabbits* by Leo Lioni to make rabbits out of wallpaper scraps.
[5–10 min.]

Internet Site: Rabbit Maze

http://members.aol.com/RainboLand/mazes.htm

Print out the maze and help the rabbit get to the end of the rainbow. May be given as a take-home activity. Site from Avstar Publishing/Rainbow Land.

Additional Resources to Share

Books

Bornstein, Ruth. *Rabbit's Good News.* Clarion, 1995. Rabbit leaves her den only to discover that spring has come.

Jeram, Anita. *Bunny, My Honey.* Candlewick, 1999. How bunny loves his mommy, and his mommy loves him in this gentle, reassuring book.

Wellington, Monica. *Night Rabbits.* Dutton, 1995. Simple text and illustrations depict the nighttime activities of young rabbits.

CD-ROM

Adventures of Peter Rabbit and Benjamin Bunny. Mindscape. Hear the stories and then play "Concentration" with cabbages. [stories, games]

The Rabbits at Home. Reed Interactive. Explore the rabbit's English country home throughout the day. [interactive activities]

Wiggle Works. Apple Home Learning/Scholastic. Listen to the story "Rabbit's Party." [stories]

Internet Sites

Disney's Daily Blast: Alice's Amazing Maze
www.disney.com/kids/DisneyBlast/alicemaze/index.html
Solve Alice's Amazing Maze and help her find the White Rabbit.

patterns for rabbit nametag or coloring sheet

Zoo Doings

Setting the Scene: Wild About Animals

Introduce the concept of caring for wild animals in zoos by using a factual book such as *Zoo* by Gail Gibbons (Crowell, 1987). Make a list with the children of all the animals that are found at the zoo in the book.
[4 min.]

CD-ROM: *The Escape of Marvin the Ape*

Watch the story of Marvin, an ape who escapes the zoo and goes to New York. Vroom Books–T/Maker.
[6 Min.]

The Zoo

The zoo has lots of animals inside.
(make circle with arms)
So unlock the doors and open them wide.
(open arms)
Elephants, tigers, lions, and bears
(hold up one finger for each animal)
Are some of the animals that are there.
(make circle with arms again)
[Fingerplay—I min.]

Book: *Counting Zoo: A Pop Up Number Book*

Big, colorful, pop-up numbers help kids find and count animals on the pages and under flaps. By Lynette Ruschak. Macmillan, 1992.
[4 min.]

Tiger

(Tune of "B-I-N-G-O")

There was a zoo that had a pet
And Tiger was his name-o.
T-I-G-E-R
T-I-G-E-R
T-I-G-E-R
And Tiger was his name-o.
(repeat with other animals such as panda, rhino, hippo, whale, snake, or zebra)
[Song—2 min.]

Game: Walking to the Zoo

Two children start this game. One person is a monkey, the other is a person. They stand on opposite sides of the room and act out the following as the other children recite the chant below.

As I Was Walking

As I was walking to the zoo one day
One brown monkey passed going the other way.
(child who is monkey walks like a monkey)
"Cheep," said the monkey.
"Hello," said I.
"Cheep, cheep," said the monkey
Then we both said "Goodbye."
(repeat with various animals and sounds until all children have a chance to participate)
[5 min.]

Zoo Sounds

(Make animal sounds after each line.)
I'm a bear—I growl.
I'm a lion—I roar.
I'm a snake—I hiss.
I'm an elephant—I trumpet.
I'm a monkey—I cheep.
I'm a rabbit—I just wiggle.
I'm a child—I wiggle.
[Rhyme—I min.]

Video: *Goodnight, Gorilla*

Pied Piper. Based on the book by Peggy Rathmann. This sparsely worded video begins when a zookeeper says goodnight to a crafty gorilla. The gorilla takes the zoo keys and follows the zoo keeper, setting loose creatures after the zoo keeper bids them goodnight.
[8 min.]

Additional Resources to Share

Books

Gibbons, Gail. *Zoo.* Crowell, 1987. Provides a behind-the-scenes look at a working day at the zoo, from the moment the workers arrive until the night guard locks the gate.

Hendrick, Mary. *If Anything Ever Goes Wrong at the Zoo.* Harcourt Brace, 1996. A young girl receives a series of zoo animals at her house after some mishaps at the zoo.

Karim, Roberta. *This Is a Hospital, Not a Zoo!* Clarion, 1998. Hospital patient Filibert Macfee transforms himself into a number of different zoo animals in order to avoid some unpleasant hospital procedures.

McPhail, David. *Animals A to Z.* Scholastic, 1988. An artists rendering of at least one animal for each letter of the alphabet.

CD-ROM

Kid's Zoo. Queue Software. Play the "Who Made That Sound?" animal matching game, which has sound and video. [factual information, games]

Zoo Explorers. Roaming Mouse Entertainment/ Compton New Media. Click on the path for Splash the Penguin and play either "The Sound and Question Game" or "Who Is It?" [factual information, games]

Internet Sites

Animals You Can See at the Zoo
www.pacificnet.net/~cmoore/zoo/index.htm
This is a story about different animals you see at the zoo. Contains animated illustrations and sounds. By Rolando Merino.

Electronic Zoo
http://netvet.wustl.edu/e-zoo.htm
Created by a veterinarian, this site has information on pets and the zoo. Site by Ken Boschert, DMV.

Naturalia: Zoo in the Wild
www.naturalia.org/zoo/welcome.html
Visit this virtual zoo in Italy that has over 150 animals and their sounds.

Rainy Day Resource Page: Zoo Animal Coloring Book
www.cp.duluth.mn.us/~sarah/rdr012.html
Pictures of zoo animals to print and color.

Multimedia Index

A

A to Zap 14

Adventures of Peter Rabbit and Benjamin Bunny 88

Adventures with Oslo: Tools and Gadgets 58

@dver@ctive: Lickety-Splat! Eat flies! 45

Alistair and the Alien Invasion Storybook 80

All the Colors of the Earth 46

Allie's Playhouse 80

Alligators All Around 16

Alligators: Appetite to Zigzag! 16

Alpha Betty and Friends 47

Alphabet Express 14

Amazing Animals 16

Ambrosia Software: Bubble Trouble 28

American Heritage Children's Dictionary 20

American Heritage Children's Dictionary Multimedia Edition 16

Animal Parade 13

Animals You Can See at the Zoo 90

Animated Sign Language Dictionary. 76

Ant and the Grasshopper 17

Apple Corps 22

ASL Spelling Study: The Alphabet 76

Astrosoft: BZZZ! 48

Athabascan Birch Bark Basket 66

Australian National Botanical Gardens: Australia's Flag 25

Awesome Animated Monster Maker 67

B

Bando Elementary School: Symphony of Friendship 47

Bat Conservation International: New Bat Facts 51

Bell on a Deer 21

Big Bug Alphabet Book 18

Biolab: Fly 45

Birmingham Zoo: American Alligators 16

Blinky Bill's Ghost Cave 25

Blue Tortoise 86

Boy, a Dog, and a Frog 48

Brian Wildsmith's Wild Animals 60

Britt Alcroft Company: Thomas and Friends 83

Bry-Back Manor Butterfly Activity Page 33

Bubblegum Machine. 29

Buckman Elementary School: Space ABCs 79

Bug Adventure 35

Bug in the Program 35

Busy People of Hamsterland 59

C

California Institute of Technology: Space Place 80

Cariboo Moose Productions: Cariboo Kids 21

Carol Moore: Buzzy Bee Online Story 35

Cat and Canary 27

Caterpillar and the Polliwog 33

Centre for Visual Sciences: B-Eye 34

Chateau Meddybemps: Fun with Trains 83

Chicka Chicka Boom Boom 13, 14

Children's Television Workshop
Big Bird's ABCs 14
Sesame Street Alphabet 13

Colgate Palmolive: Dr. Rabbit's No Cavity Clubhouse 81

Come to the Playroom 43

Contra Costa County Office of Education: Bat Flip Book 50

Curious George's ABC Adventure 14

Cuthbert the Caterpillar 32

Cybermom: Alphabet 14

D

Dark, Dark Tale 67

David's Whale & Dolphin Watch 37

Dental Website 59

Destination Rainforest 61

Dia de los Muertos 31

Discovery.com: The Ultimate Guide to Ants 18

Disney's Active Play: It's a Bug's Life 18

Disney's Daily Blast: Alice's Amazing Maze 88

Dole 5-a-Day Adventure 23

Dole Food Company: Just for Kids 23

Dolphins, Our Friends from the Sea 38

Dr. T's Sing-A-Long Around the World 63

E

EarthQuest: Polar Trek 70

Electronic Zoo 90

Elroy Goes Bugzerk 35

Elves and the Shoemaker 64

Emmett Scott's Cartoon Corner: Help Peetie Count the Flies 45

Encarta Multimedia Encyclopedia 36

Enchanted Learning Software
All About Alligators 16
All About Birds 27
The Ants Go Marching 18
Bee Rhyme 34
Egg Carton Animals 51
"Fiddle Dee Dee" 45
Humpty Dumpty 40
Little Explorers Picture Bee Rhyme 34
There Was an Old Lady Who Swallowed a Fly 44
This Little Piggy 73
Zoom School Australia 25

Encyclopedia of Cajun Culture 36

Escape of Marvin the Ape 89

Everyday Cajun Homepage 36

Exploratorium: Professor Bubble's Bubblesphere 29

Eyewitness Children's Encyclopedia. 18

F

Farm Animals for Windows 43

Fisher Price Pirate Ship 74

Fiona Neary of Heritage Studios: Three

Key to the Index

Website names appear in plain type   **CD-ROM titles appear in bold type**

Video titles appear in italic type

Little Pigs 72
Fisher Price: Games and Activities 59
Flipper Interactive Story Book 38
Forever Growing Garden 55
Four Footed Friends 47
Franklin Institute: Heart Preview Gallery 57
Franklin's Reading World 86
Frog and Toad Are Friends 48
Froggy Page 49
Funschool Corporation: Haunted Alphabet 67

G

Games in Spanish 31
GE Research and Development: Three Dimensional Medical Reconstruction 57
GooboWorks: Build a Monster 67
Goodnight, Gorilla 89
Grace Bell Collection 26
Granny Applebee's Cookie Factory 23
Green Eggs and Ham 40

H

Happy Saint Patricks Rainbow Coloring Page 64
Heard Elementary School Library: Looney Lobster's Travel Journal 36
Hedgehog Review: All About Hedgehogs 53
Hedgehogs.net 53
HomeAts.com: Hedgehog Movie 52
Honey Bee: A Profile 35
Honey.com: Kids 35
Hoot and Kat "Best Friends" 47
Hot-Cha-Cha! Activities 30

I

I Know an Old Lady 44
I Like Science: Butterflies and Moths. 33
I Love Sunflowers 55
Iceblox 71
Iguana Images: IguanaCam 62
Infostuff: Alphabet of Animals 13
Inner Learning Online: Human Anatomy Online 56
Interactive Sign Language: Fingerspelling and Numbers 76
Internet Library: The Tortoise and the Hare 87
Introduction to the Amniota 39
Isabelle in Mexico—Visiting the Mayas 31

J

Johnny Appleseed 23
Johnny Appleseed Inc.: Johnny Appleseed Home Page 23
Juegos y Canciones para los Niños 30
Jump Start Spanish 31
Junior Nature Guides: Birds 27

K

Kevin the Kangaroo 25
Kid's Domain
    Adopt a Rainforest Animal 60
    Bubble Puzzle 28
Kid's Zoo 90
Kids & Careers Website 59
Kids Count Entertainment: One Seed Can Make a Difference 54
Kids on Site 59
Kids Valley Garden 55
Kidshealth.org: How the Body Works 57
Kidstory Series: The Little Engine That Could 83
KidsTV: Make a Pirate Hat 74
Kidz Corner: Sea Turtles for Kids 86

L

Let's Be Friends 46
Let's Explore the Farm 43
Let's Explore the Jungle 61
Let's Give Kitty a Bath 29
Little Red Hen 59, 73
Lizard! Lizards! Lizards! 62
Louisiana History: The Louisiana Legacy 36
LouisianaRadio: Cajun Music 36
Love Flute 66
Luke Saves the Day 74

M

Magic Apple House 23
Magic School Bus Gets Lost in Space 80
Magic School Bus: Gets Ants in Its Pants 18
Magic School Bus: Inside Ralphie 57
Magic Tales Interactive Storybook 64
Magic Tales Interactive Storybook II 66
MaMaMedia.com: Presto 58
Mars Moose 21
Math Blaster 78
Me and My World 38
Melno the Frog 49
Michigan Department of Agriculture:

Kids Korner 43
Midcontinent Ecological Sciences Ctr: Children's Butterfly Site 33
Midnight Farm 43
Most Wonderful Egg in the World 39
Mr. Potato Head Saves Veggie Valley 55
Multimedia Bird Book 27
Multimedia Bug Book 33, 78
My Amazing Human Body 56, 81
My Card Shop 64
My First Amazing World Explorer 25
My First Incredible Amazing Dictionary 62
My Neighborhood 53

N

National Geographic: Dinosaur Eggs 40
Native American Arts and Crafts 66
Native American Peoples of the Plains 65
Native Americans 66
Naturalia: Zoo in the Wild 90
New Frog and Fly 45
New Jersey Online: Worm World 77
Nickelodian Jr.: Franklin Online 86
Nikolai's Train 84
Nobby Nuss Game 68

O

Once Upon a Forest 53
Owl Educational Software 43
Ozzie's Funtime Garden 55
Ozzie's Travels: Destination Mexico 31
Ozzie's World 51

P

PBS: Tots TV Tilly, Tom & Tiny Puppets 46
Paws Signs Stories 76
Peanut Butter 68
Peanuts Picture Puzzler 69
Penguin Links 71
Penguin Page 70
Penny Penguin's Math Bingo 71
Pirate Who Would Not Wash 74
Pittsburgh Zoo: Kangaroo Pictures and Information 25
Places for Kids Online 59
Planet Zoom: Vegetable Head Game 55
Planter's Company: Relax and Go Nuts 69

Playground of Friends 47
Polar Express 84
Powerup. com: Luke Saves the Day 74
Putt Putt Goes to the Moon 80

Q

Quick Learn Software: The Beekeepers
    Home Page 35

R

Rabbit Maze 87
Rabbits at Home 88
Rainforest Action Network: The
    Rainforest 61
Rainforest Alliance: For Kids and
    Teachers 61
Rainy Day Resource Page: Zoo Animal
    Coloring Book 90
Red Bluff Ranch: Kid's Farm 43
Rene Romeg's African Pigmy Hedgehog
    Page 53
Richard Scarry's Best Video Ever 14
Richard Scarry's How Things Work in
    Busytown 59
Round Bird Can't Fly 26
Royal British Columbia Museum: Grace
    Bell Collection 26

S

Safety Scavenger Hunt 74
Sammy's Science House 85
Scary Squirrel World: Nobby Nuss Game
    68
Science Museum of Minnesota
    Bubble Geometry 29
    Monarch Page 32
    Thinking Fountain 40
Sea Creatures 38
Sea Creatures Mystery Game 37
Sea Turtle Adventures 86
Sea World: Dolphin and Me Coloring
    Page 38
Seaside Adventure 38
Sesame Street Numbers 50

Shade's Landing: Heather's Happy St.
    Patricks Day 63
Shelly Duvall's It's a Bird's Life 27, 69
Sign Language for Everyone 76
Sign Language Page 76
Sing N Sign for Fun 76
Sitting on a Farm 41
Slimy Frog Software: Koji the Frog 49
Snail's Race Game 78
Southern Living: Rudolph
    Cookies/Magic Reindeer Food 21
Space Worms 78
Squigly's Playhouse: Turtle Coloring
    Sheet 85
St. Louis Zoo: Babirusa 72
Stamped on Fairy Tales: Pigs 72
Stardom Company: Barnyard Buddies 41
Stellaluna 51
Students for the Exploration and
    Development of Space 80
Swamp Gas USA 36

T

Thinkquest: Pirates! 74
Titch 55
Tomorrow's Promise Spelling 49
Tooth Fairy 82
Tooth Fairy Page 82
Tooth Fairy Tales: Bad Breath Invasion
    82
Traditional Native American "Hidden
    Ball" Game 66
Travelrama 36
True Friends Have Fun: The Magic Berry
    Patch 21
Turtle Coloring Sheet 85
12 Hedgehogs Puzzle Game 52
Twentieth Century Fox: Casper's Ghost
    Cards 67

U

UC Berkeley: Introduction to the
    Amniota 39
UC Santa Cruz Dept. of Biology: Video
    Lizards 62

University of Ulm: Interactive Model
    Railroad 84
University Park Elementary School:
    Moose Tales 20
Urban Programs Resource Network: The
    Adventures of Herman 78

V

*Very Hungry Caterpillar and Other
    Stories 62*
VirtualKiss.com: E-Shamrocks 64

W

Walnuts Game 69
Wangaratta Primary School 25
Washington State Apple Commission:
    Apple Cards 23
Water Works Balloon Bundle 29
Welcome to Bodyland 57
Whale Club Coloring Book 38
What Is a Bellybutton? 57, 82
What's the Secret? 35
Where Did My Toothbrush Go? 82
Wiggle Works 88
Wildlife Preservation Trust International:
    The Wild Ones 15
Wild Sanctuary 15
Wilderness Society: Deer Coloring Sheet
    21
Winslow Press: Hot-Cha-Cha! Activities
    30
World of Animals 39
World of Animals: Butterflies 33
World of Plants 22
World of Totty Pig: You Are Much
    Too Small 73
World Walker: Destination Australia
    24

Z

Zoo Explorers 29, 90
Zoo-opolis 52
Zurk's Rainforest Lab 40, 60